The Champion Edge

The Champion Edge

Skill Sets That Fire Up Your Business and Life

Alan R. Zimmerman

BEP

BUSINESS EXPERT PRESS

Leader in applied, concise business books

The Champion Edge: Skill Sets That Fire Up Your Business and Life

Copyright © Business Expert Press, LLC, 2021.

Cover design by Charlene Kronstedt

Interior design by Exeter Premedia Services Private Ltd., Chennai, India

First published in 2021 by
Business Expert Press, LLC
222 East 46th Street, New York, NY 10017
www.businessexpertpress.com

ISBN-13: 978-1-95334-982-8 (paperback)
ISBN-13: 978-1-95334-983-5 (e-book)

Business Expert Press Business Career Development Collection

Collection ISSN: 2642-2123 (print)
Collection ISSN: 2642-2131 (electronic)

First edition: 2021

10 9 8 7 6 5 4 3 2 1

To my wife, Chris, who has always loved me, believed in me, and brought out my best. Her faith, intellect, courage, and strength have made my life and work so much more fun, exciting, and meaningful

Description

Without question, some people accomplish so much more than others in their careers and their lives. And they do it so much more quickly. Surprisingly, there is nothing in the research that adequately accounts for this difference in success, except one thing. The most successful people invariably practice three skill sets that give them a distinct, get-ahead, accelerated edge at work and at home. It's called *The Champion Edge* and is comprised of *purpose, passion,* and *process,* all of which can be learned, adopted, and mastered by the reader.

This book gives specific skills and step-by-step strategies that will empower the reader to clarify their purpose, align *their* life and career with that purpose, build a more positive attitude, remain persistent, make decisions guided by character, achieve goals through the use of affirmations, communicate more effectively, and listen to what is said and left unsaid.

Keywords

success; career success; business career; career development; personal development; professional development; purpose; discovering your purpose; attitude; positive attitude; positive thinking; negative thinking; passion; persistence; ethics; character; goal setting; goal achievement; affirmations; communication; interpersonal communication; effective communication; listening; improving listening; winner; champion; success strategies

Contents

Acknowledgments

To any of you who have ever written a book or contemplated doing so, you know that a book doesn't just happen or magically appear on the pages of a computer document. Most of the time, it is the result of years and years of learning and time-tested experience, *and* the input of several significant people in the author's life.

In fact, without certain people in my life and work, this book may not have been written, or written quite as well. I want to thank a few of those people here.

To my father, mother, and stepmother: I have never known a day without your unconditional love and support. What a rare and awesome blessing! You believed in me before I believed in myself.

To the three teachers who carved a lasting legacy in my life—Virgelee LeDue, Sally Webb, and Sidney Simon: you did so much more than teach a class. You demonstrated professionalism, demanded excellence, cared deeply, and, even more incredibly, stayed in contact with me for decades after I left your classrooms.

To the hundreds of thousands of people who have read and followed my weekly Internet newsletter, *Dr. Zimmerman's Tuesday Tips,* for many years: your continual flow of encouraging handwritten notes and electronic e-mails made my day, day after day after day.

To the 3,000+ audiences where I have spoken around the world, and to the hundreds of organizations who have extended me *"the privilege of the platform,"* giving me the opportunity to share what I've learned with your people, I am honored beyond words. Together we have made a huge and positive difference in the lives and careers of countless people.

CHAPTER 1

What Does a Champion Look Like?

Two questions have bugged me all my life.

First, why do some people accomplish so much more than others in their business careers and lives? And second, why do some people accomplish so much more than others … so much more quickly?

I have spent decades researching the answers to those two questions and sharing what I've learned with my students at the University of Minnesota and more than 3,000 audiences in various businesses where I have delivered keynotes and seminars. I think you're going to be surprised as well as delighted by the answers I've found.

The surprising part is there is nothing in the research that adequately accounts for this difference in success. It cannot be explained by age, birth order, gender, education, race, religion, ethnic identity, nationality, sexual orientation, political philosophy, economic circumstances, or any other known factor.

The delightful part is the most successful people invariably practice certain skill sets that you can learn. And these skill sets will fire up the success of your business career and life. That's why it's called *The Champion Edge* (TCE). They will give you a distinct, get ahead, accelerated edge at work and at home.

But let's get our terminology straight before you apply these three skills sets.

A Winner or a Champion?

Most of the research is focused on becoming a winner. You know, the motivational research, sports psychology, and the like.

The dictionary defines a champion as "one who wins first place or first prize in a competition" or "a person who has defeated or surpassed all rivals in a competition." I disagree. That's the definition of a "winner."

A champion is so much more than a person who comes in first place. After all, you know lots of "winners" who have come in first place at something, who have achieved fame and fortune, but are bankrupt as human beings.

I also dislike that definition of a champion. If it's all about being a "winner," it implies that there has to be a loser, perhaps lots of losers. In reality, everyone who adopts the three skills sets of *The Champion Edge* can become a champion.

A champion is much bigger and better and more effective, productive, and positive than a mere "winner" could ever be. As Lee Labrada, the former bodybuilding IFBB Mr. Universe and the founder of Labrada Nutrition, says, "A champion is not *someTHING* you become by winning a major bodybuilding title or any other athletic event. A champion is *someBODY* you become by walking a never-ending path of self-improvement."

Great words. They give us a beginning glimpse of what a champion looks like.

But let me take that a step further. From my research and experience with countless numbers of champions, I've discovered that true champions are characterized by seven behaviors that give them an edge in their business careers and lives. *The Champion Edge.*

Let's take a quick look at those seven behaviors here. And as you read through these behaviors, it would be worthwhile for you to score yourself on each of the behaviors, from 1 to 10, with 10 being the best, most positive score.

Seven Characteristics of a Champion

A Champion Has a Positive Attitude

Champions know that their attitude is their most important asset. They know that it is their attitude at the beginning of any task, which, more than anything else, will affect its successful outcome.

After all, a good attitude brings good results and a bad attitude brings bad results. I would even say that nothing on this planet has a greater influence on who you become or the success you achieve than your attitude.

What about you? Do you have a positive attitude toward your future, your career, and your life? Many people don't. Many people are dead at 30 but don't get buried until they're 75.

On a scale of 1 to 10, with 10 being the best, how would you rate your overall attitude? If you have anything less than a 7, your chances of being a champion in your business career or your chances of being a champion in your relationships are very low.

No matter what score you give yourself, I'll show you exactly how you build and maintain an attitude that is positive, productive, and profitable later in this book. It's one of the three skill sets of a champion, the skill set of passion.

For the moment, however, you need to know that a champion's positive attitude has at least two components: *self-esteem* and *enthusiasm*. They believe in themselves and they're filled with energy.

Self-esteem is not some esoteric, touchy-feely concept that has no impact on your life and results. Not at all. It has critical bottom-line consequences because you perform exactly as you see yourself. If you can see yourself as confident, optimistic, and achieving your goals, you're on the path to success. But if you can't even imagine yourself holding a C-level position in an organization, you're dead before you start.

This might sound a little strange, talking about your self-esteem in a business-career accelerating book. But I believe they are deeply interconnected. As novelist Doris Mortman asserts, "Until you make peace with who you are, you will never be content with what you have."[1]

The *enthusiasm* part of a positive attitude is the fuel you need to get ahead in your career and life. As filmmaker and producer George Lucas describes it, "You have to find something that you love enough to be able to take risks, jump over the hurdles and break through the brick walls that are always going to be placed in front of you. If you don't have that kind of feeling for what it is you are doing, you'll stop at the first giant hurdle."

Of course, some people will tell me that they're just not the energetic, passionate type. They mistakenly think they could never have the enthusiasm they need to be highly successful in their lives, careers, and relationships.

That's baloney. That's ignorance talking. A person can learn to be enthusiastic. I teach people how to do that every day. And you'll learn that as well in in this book.

A Champion Is Goal-Focused

The connection between goal-setting and higher levels of achievement is indisputable. People who have clear, specific, written goals almost always accomplish a great deal more than people who never bother to think about their goals, write them down, and plan them out. Champions know that and act accordingly.

Unfortunately, only a small percentage of people are actually goal-focused. They prefer to "wing it" or "keep their options open."

What about you? Do you have clear, specific, and written goals for today, this week, this month, this year, and the next five, 10, and 15 years? Do you have those kinds of goals for your business career, your life, and relationships? If not, it's almost a certainty that you'll end up somewhere you don't want to be.

Again, if you're not pleased with your answer, no problem. I'll address this in detail in another section of this book, the second skill set of champions, known as the skill set of process.

When you are goal-focused, you get *direction*. It puts a target, or several targets, in your career and life. It tells you what direction to take so you don't get sidetracked.

You also get *persistence*. Major General Charles C. Noble, an engineer who developed the early American intercontinental ballistic missiles (ICBM) program, learned that firsthand. He said, "You must have long-range goals to keep you from being frustrated by short-range failures."[2]

A Champion Is Action-Oriented

Conrad Hilton, the founder of the Hilton Hotel chain, said, "Achievement seems to be connected with action. Successful men and women keep moving."[3]

Absolutely! Champions don't wait for things to happen in their careers or lives. They don't wait for success to fall in their laps, and they don't wait for their lottery ticket to be chosen. They take action. They keep on doing the things that will get them closer and closer to their desired goals.

As author, professor, and coach David J. Schwartz says, champions know that "Dreams are fulfilled only through action, not through endless planning to take action."[4]

In particular, champions do not procrastinate. They take action now. They know some moments are better than others for action, but there is never a perfect moment. So they do it ... *now* ... if at all possible ... and if at all sensible.

By contrast, non-champions put things off. Physician and athlete George Sheehan described such people when he said, "There are those of us who are always about to live. We are waiting until things change, until there is more time, until we are less tired, until we get a promotion, until we settle down—until, until, until. It always seems as if there is some major event that must occur in our lives before we begin living."[5]

Such behavior is *not* what *The Champion Edge* is all about! We'll go into more detail on being action-oriented in the passion skill set a little later in this book.

Until you get there, keep these two thoughts in mind. First, you don't have to be great to start, but you have to start to be great.

And second, adhere to the wisdom of the unknown source who said, "Twenty years from now, you will be more disappointed by the things you didn't do than by the ones you did do. So throw off the bowlines. Sail away from the safe harbor. Catch the trade winds in your sails. Explore. Dream. Discover."

A Champion Takes Constructive Risks

A champion knows success seldom falls upon the faint of heart or the lily-livered cowards. That's why management guru Peter Drucker says, "In every success story, you find someone who has made a courageous decision."

Dr. Maxwell Maltz documented that in his book, *Psycho-Cybernetics*. He said, "Often the difference between a successful person and a failure is not the one that has better abilities or ideas, but the courage that one has to bet on one's ideas, to take a calculated risk—and to act."[6]

Champions are "what's next" people.
Non-champions are "what if" people.

Non-champions live smaller lives and have less successful careers because they're constantly plagued by the "what if's." What if the stock market goes down or Social Security is not there to help them when they retire? What if their company merges with another and they lose their job? What if they have to keep on working with a difficult boss or team member? What if they decide to marry someone and it doesn't work out?

Plagued by fear and the "what if's," non-champions stay in their comfort zones. They don't realize that everything they want more of—better health, a better relationship, a better job, a better financial portfolio, everything—lies outside their comfort zone.

Simply put, champions take more risks—constructive risks—because they know life is either a matter or risk or regret.

Where do you fit in the continuum? Are you more of a "what's next" person or a "what if" person? It will make a huge difference in your outcomes.

A Champion Overcomes Obstacles

Champions know there are very few if any "overnight successes." So they persevere. They relentlessly pursue their goals, endure hardship, walk away from distractions, turn away from temptations, and doggedly maintain their focus on the things they desire. All of that means they overcome obstacles.

Indeed, all champions talk about this characteristic. Booker T. Washington, a former slave and later a prominent educator, wrote, "I have learned that success is to be measured not so much by the position that one has reached in life as by the obstacles which he has had to overcome while trying to succeed."[7]

A few years later, the genius inventor and prominent businessman Thomas Edison echoed the same sentiment. He said, "Our greatest weakness lies in giving up. The most certain way to succeed is always to try just one more time."

One of the main reasons champions are champions is they do what most people don't feel like doing. They overcome the inevitable obstacles that pop up in their careers and lives, whether or not they feel like it.

What about you? How often do you let yourself off the hook? How guilty are you of giving up when obstacles appear? How often do you use such statements as "I don't want to" or "I just don't feel like it?"

I know I was guilty of that years ago, until my mentor and first boss, John Weiner, the president of the Weiner Shoe Company, challenged me. He asked, "Alan, do you like pleasing habits or pleasing results?"

As I pondered that probing question, and squirmed in my chair like a worm at the end of a hook, I knew I had been doing it all wrong. I was "saying" that I was interested in pleasing *results*—like a close relationship with my kids. But I was more focused on the easy things, the pleasing *habits*—like buying the kids a bunch of stuff—rather than spend quality time with them. I was doing what pleased me, what I felt like doing, when I felt like doing it, and then complained about how things never seemed to work out for me.

A few moments later, I answered, "I like pleasing results." From that day on, my life changed. I began to do the things that needed to be done—whether or not I felt like it. I became an obstacle overcomer. And you will too with the strategies you learn in the champion skill set of passion later in this book.

Champions Hold Themselves Accountable

Indeed, accountability has been one of the most popular business buzz words of the last several years. Apparently because there has been either a lack of it or a misunderstanding of it.

Not so with a champion. Champions understand the critical importance of accountability in accelerating their business career success. And they act accordingly.

To be more precise, when I've worked with champions, I've noticed that their accountability is always characterized by four subcomponents.

- **Performance**
  Champions know that it doesn't matter how hard they try or how good their intentions are. They know that in the real world the only thing that counts is performance. As Harold S. Geneen, the former CEO of ITT, put it, "Performance is your reality. Forget everything else."[8]

- **Responsibility**

  When champions win, they give themselves credit for their successes. And when they lose, they don't blame others for their shortcomings or make excuses for their setbacks. They take responsibility for their failures.

- **Learning**

  The very essence of becoming a champion is connected to education. They look for the lesson in every success and every failure, so they can repeat what works and avoid what doesn't. They intentionally pursue whatever formal or informal education that will give them more of The Champion Edge. That kind of learning and accountability is attached to an openness to feedback. Champions want to know how well they're doing and how they can get even better. They take on the Winston Churchill attitude, who said, "I am always ready to learn, but I do not always like to be taught."

- **Modeling**

  In addition to holding themselves accountable for the work they do, champions also hold themselves accountable for the example they set. As Labrada declares, "Like it or not, a champion is a role model for others. A champion lives his life correctly, knowing that others will be watching and emulating him. The world is full of superstar athletes that live lives of debauchery and excess. They are not to be confused for champions. If it weren't for their God-given talent, they would be losers."

How would you rate yourself in terms of accountability? If you have some room for improvement, if you need more of the four accountability subcomponents I just mentioned, you'll find several strategies in champion edge skill sets known as passion and purpose.

A Champion Cares about Others

A winner may not.

Perhaps you remember the woman who hopped on a subway during the Boston Marathon. No big deal, except for one detail. She was supposed to be running the marathon! Later, witnesses saw her jump into the race less than a mile from the finish line. She finished well ahead of all the other female runners, and oddly, she wasn't winded or even sweating much. For a brief time, she looked like the winner.

But she wasn't a champion. A winner might come in first through cheating, connections, and unethical shortcuts. And even though the world might see her as a winner, she would definitely not be a champion because her focus would be on herself rather than caring about others.

Champions know that a great deal of their personal and professional success will come from building relationships with others—relationships based on genuine care and concern for the people with whom they work and live. They follow the old Chinese proverb that says, "If you want 1 year of prosperity, grow grain. If you want 10 years of prosperity, grow trees. If you want 100 years of prosperity, grow people." Or to put it my way, grow caring relationships.

To a hard-nosed, data-driven businessperson, caring might sound too soft to be of any practical use. I disagree for three reasons.

- *First, caring paves the way for effective communication.* As the saying goes, "No one cares how much you know until they know how much you care." That only makes sense. Why would anyone want to hear you talk or why would anyone want to listen to what you have to say if they're not convinced that you care about them?
- *Second, caring builds the foundation for cooperation and teamwork.* As my mentor and best-selling author Zig Ziglar said millions of times, "You can have everything in life you want, if you will just help other people get what they want."
- *Third, caring shifts the focus from "me" to "we."* And that alone is the very premise on which successful businesses are built and extraordinary customer service is delivered.

I remember when that shift happened in my career. As a young entrepreneur, business owner, and professional speaker, I was constantly focused on how I could get more business, how I could make more money, and how I could get more publicity. I, I, I. Me, me, me. And that did bring a measure of success. I was a winner but not a champion.

The shift came when I heard Arnold "Red" Auerbach, the great American basketball coach and executive, say the following, "Take pride in what you do. The kind of pride I'm talking about is not the arrogant puffed-up kind; it's just the whole idea of caring—fiercely caring."

My mindset changed from thinking I was so cool, great, and wonderful—that I was gift to my audiences. I began thinking, before I walked on stage, "There they are ... my audience. What an honor, what a privilege it is to speak to them. What can I do to help them experience more happiness and success?"

The results were staggering. Within a short time, I was inducted into the Speaker Hall of Fame, along with President Ronald Reagan, General Colin Powell, Executive Chairman of the Great Harvest Bread Company, Nido Qubein, and best-selling authors Ken Blanchard and Jack Canfield. My move toward champion status had been validated.

To help you nail down this caring characteristic, pay special attention to *The Champion Edge* skill set in this book called process.

Conclusion

Earlier I raised the question as to why some people accomplish so much more than others? So much more quickly. You know the answer. They are champions. They exhibit the seven characteristics we just discussed.

But how do you get there? What skills are needed? What do you have to do? You have to master three skill sets: purpose, passion, and process. Those three skills sets, put together, put into practice will give you *The Champion Edge* to fire up the success of your business career and life.

Read on. I'm excited to be taking this journey with you.

CHAPTER 2

What Gives You the Champion Edge (TCE)?

Three Skill Sets

It's obvious that some people accomplish so much more than others. And they do it so much more quickly than others. You've seen them, perhaps know them, have worked with them, or at least heard about them. There are champions among us. And I suspect you're either a champion or want to become one.

In the last chapter I outlined the seven characteristics of a champion. I alluded to the fact that they became that way because they have *The Champion Edge (TCE)* working for them. And you get *TCE* when you learn, practice, master, and apply all three skill sets. That's what this book is all about.

The three skill sets are purpose, passion, and process. They are the how-to's that turn your effort into meaningful outcomes. They are the how-to's that turn your performance into peak performance. They are the how-to's that bring out your best so you are the best in your business career and life.

As such, this is a *prescriptive* book. I'm going to share dozens of skills and strategies and tips and tactics that have proven to work with countless people. I'm going to tell you what works.

And this is an *action* book. I'm going to push you to do certain things so you excel in the areas of purpose, passion, and process. Because reading this book will do very little for you. But applying this book will give you *The Champion Edge* that will accelerate your career and life.

So let's take a moment to briefly define each of the three skill sets that comprise *TCE*. That way you'll know where we're headed. And then the rest of the book will be totally focused on making those skills a reality for you.

Purpose is all about the *where* and *why* questions. Where do you want to go with your career and life? Why do you want that? Why is that important to you? Champions have clear answers for those questions.

Passion is all about the *how* question. How are you going to keep on keeping on? How will you get enough fuel for the long-haul career success you desire? And how will you know you're on the right path? Champions are known for their passion.

Process is all about the *what* question. What do you have to do to accomplish your goals, not only for yourself but with others? Champions master certain intra and interpersonal communication skills.

The *Purpose* Skill Set

Over the last several years, books on "the power of purpose" and having a "purpose-driven life" have been among the best-sellers in history. Hundreds of millions of people have been desperately hoping to find their purpose or clarify their professional or personal purposes. And that makes sense. The Bible, Proverbs 29: 18 (KJV) says that "Where there is no vision, the people perish." In other words, no purpose equals no life-sustaining direction.

That's why knowing your purpose is the starting point for getting TCE working for you, because purpose gives you direction. It answers the *where* question.

Without direction, you become very much like Alice in Lewis Carroll's *Alice's Adventures in Wonderland* (London: Macmillan, 1865) who asks the Cheshire cat, "Would you please tell me which way I ought to go from here?"

"That depends on where you want to get," the cat replied. "I don't care much where," Alice answered. "Then it doesn't matter which way you go," the cat responded.

Without the direction that purpose gives you, you could possibly achieve a lot but feel empty inside, wondering what's the point of all your hard work.

Purpose gives you the *where* you're going and the *why* you're going there. Debbi Fields, the founder of Mrs. Fields' Cookies, demonstrated that. Even though she was labeled an "empty-headed housewife" who had to fight bankers, family members, friends, vendors, and suppliers who tried to run and ruin her life and business, she had *TCE* because her purpose was clear. She said, "I've never felt like I was in the cookie business. I've always been in a feel-good business. My job is to sell joy. My job is to sell happiness. My job is to sell an experience."

Without purpose, your career and life will be more like that of a human lobster than a champion. More inert than alert.

You see, when a lobster is left high and dry among the rocks, he doesn't exert the energy to work his way back into the sea. He waits for the sea to come to him. If it doesn't come, he just sits there and dies, although the slightest effort would get him back into ocean, which is perhaps a yard away. As author Dr. Orrison Swett Marden wrote, "The world is full of human lobsters: Men stranded on the rocks of indecision and procrastination, who instead of putting forth their own energies, are waiting for some grand billow of good fortune to set them afloat."[1]

With purpose, however, you don't wait for things to happen. You make them happen. As Canadian naval officer and senator, Douglas Everett, said, "There are some people, who live in a dream world, and there are some people who face reality ... and then there are some who turn one into another."[2] Champions do that. They turn their purpose or dreams into reality. I'll show you how in the next chapter.

The *Passion* Skill Set

Passion or self-motivation is a critical part of *TCE*, the fuel part or the *how* you're going to reach your destination. Sir Edmund Hillary, the first person to climb Mt. Everest, exemplified that. When asked about his amazing accomplishment, he replied, "You don't have to be a fantastic hero to do certain things. You can be just an ordinary chap, *sufficiently motivated* to reach challenging goals."

What percentage of the time are you *sufficiently motivated*? Later in the book, I'll give you a number of strategies you can use to keep yourself motivated and on the right track.

I'll give you a sneak peek, however. One part of *TCE* passion is an *"it's-up-to-me"* attitude. It might sound cute or even trite. The kind of rally cry you might hear from a rah-rah motivational speaker. But it's not some light fluffy statement that you can afford to dismiss.

Champions know that no one gave them a bad attitude and no one can give them a good attitude. And you need to realize "it's up to me." No one is responsible for your success—not your boss, your company, your husband, your wife, your parents, or anybody else—except you. Oh sure, those other people can help, support, and encourage you, but none of them can make you successful. You are responsible for your success. And a champion with passion accepts responsibility for getting and keeping that kind of motivation.

David Adkins, better known as the actor Sinbad, understands that. He says, "My mother and father taught me everything: integrity, honesty, being responsible. My father told me you can't be great at anything unless you accept responsibility."

In fact, those who dismiss this *"it's-up-to-me"* attitude end up in trouble. It's why the vast majority of Americans reaching retirement age lack the financial resources to take care of their basic needs—without some form of government help. They never fully understood the fact that it was up to them, not the government or their company to secure their future.

It's why so many people never seem to move ahead in their lives, their careers, or their relationships. They don't buy or read educational books, and they don't invest their own time and money into motivational recordings, written materials, or seminars. They do very little to continue their growth and development and thereby increase their value to their companies and the people in their lives. And they wonder why they aren't better off today than they were last year. It's because they don't have an *"it's-up-to-me"* attitude that pushes them toward continual education.

Passion is *how* you're going to fire up your motivation, follow-through, and character that ensures the success of your business career and life.

The *Process* Skill Set

Process is the third part of *TCE*, the *what* question. What do you have to do to accomplish your goals, not only for yourself but with others? Whereas purpose and passion relate to your heart or emotional intelligence skills, process brings in your head or social intelligence skills as well. And as the late Nelson Mandela, the former president of South Africa, phrased it, "A good head and a good heart are always a formidable combination."

Fortunately, research tells us a great deal as to what process skills work and don't work so you don't have to waste your time keeping busy, trying to guess your way to champion success through trial and error. You can focus on the mental and communication skills that have proven to bring out the best in yourself and the cooperation of others. That's why novelist Ernest Hemingway said, "Never confuse motion and action." And that's why I tell my audiences, "Don't confuse activity with accomplishment."[3]

We'll focus on those exact process skills later in the book. And I can assure you they will work for you. Dr. Charles Garfield, a professor at the University of California's medical school and head of the Peak Performance Center, agrees. He says, "You have the power to change your habits of mind and acquire certain skills. And if you choose to do so, you can improve your performance, your productivity and the quality of your whole life."[4]

One of those process skills is the *"do-a-little-bit-more"* behavior. As author A. Lou Vickery summarizes it, "Four short words sum up what has lifted most successful individuals above the crowd: a little bit more. They did all that was expected of them and a little bit more."[5]

A 19th-century history professor Charles Kendall Adams put it this way, "No one ever attains very eminent success by simply doing what is required of him; it is the amount and excellence of what is over and above the required that determines the greatness of ultimate distinction."[6] In other words, a little bit more.

For example, champions know if they want to double their paycheck, they will have to do a little bit more to triple their value. When you do that, one of three things will happen. One, your present employer will respond with raises, bonuses, and promotions. Two, a new employer will find and grab you. Or three, you'll discover some way to start your own business and write your own paycheck. And if you already own a business and want to double your paycheck, simply take action to triple the value you offer your customers.

When you do that, most of the time (hey, life isn't always fair) your compensation will catch up to your value. And even if your compensation doesn't catch up as much or as fast as you would like, you'll still feel a great deal better about doing your best than doing just enough to get by.

It's Time to Stop Using Dumb Strategies

Now you know what a champion looks like. We outlined that in Chapter 1. And you also know that a champion becomes that way because he or she has *The Champion Edge* working for them: purpose, passion, and process.

So where are you right now with regard to champion status? Are you getting everything you want out of your career and your life? If so, congratulations. If not, you're in the right place.

This is the place where you stop using some dumb strategies that have almost no chance of success. This is the place where you stop doing the same things in the same ways, year after year. This is the place where you start practicing the skills that do work and make *TCE* a part of who you are, professionally and personally.

PART I

Purpose

CHAPTER 3

The Power of Purpose

Where *The Champion Edge* Begins

You have a purpose. You really do. As Native American author Christine Quintasket (1884–1936), who was also known as Mourning Dove, put it, "Everything on the earth has a purpose, every disease an herb to cure it, and every person a mission."[1]

You have a purpose and it is much bigger than merely going to work, collecting a paycheck, and paying off the mortgage. That's survival, but it's not purpose. *You* are here to make some kind of positive difference in the world. It may be in your family, your company, or your nation, but you're here to make your world a better place.

You have a purpose, and when you discover or clarify it, you answer two of the biggest questions you will ever face. *Where* do you want to go with your career and life? And *why* do you want that? You are starting to let *The Champion Edge* work for you rather than let doubt, confusion, and indecision get in your way.

You have a purpose that will empower you, if you let it. As author and Navy Seal Jeff Boss, says, "Purpose pulls. It's what compels you to *do*, to create, to explore and discover … Purpose is like a freight train in that its momentum is too difficult to stop after it's started; it's too appealing *not* to continue its pursuit after that journey has begun. Why? Because the allure of attaining purpose (whatever that means) is a powerful force."[2]

You have a purpose, and when you deploy it, you are taking one of the biggest steps you will ever take toward the success you desire. As the former British prime minister Benjamin Disraeli declared, "The secret of success is constancy of purpose."[3] In other words, purpose brings out your best. It keeps you going. It moves you beyond motivation to inspiration and into the big leagues of success.

Perhaps you've noticed something. For five paragraphs in a row, I have emphatically stated, "*You* have a purpose." That may be encouraging for you to hear but possibly frustrating. Because you may not know what your exact purpose is or how to figure it out. You may not even know why on earth you're here in the first place. You may feel like the man in England whose tombstone epitaph read, "Here lies a man who lived and died but never knew who he was."

You're not alone. A lot of people are struggling with those questions. And that's not a comfortable or profitable place to live. *Without* purpose, you will never have *TCE* working for you. And you may spend your whole life trying to climb the ladder of success to a destination that isn't worth reaching.

But please hang in there. In the next chapter I will show you exactly how to discover and/or clarify your purpose, how to write it out and then apply it to every part of your professional and personal lives. In this chapter I simply want to convince you that your purpose is way too important to ignore or skip over if you ever hope to be a champion.

Are You Living by Your Priorities or Your Pressures?

It's an important question because there are only two ways you can live and work. You can live and work with purpose, using your *priorities to create* the success you desire. Or you can live and work without purpose, letting the *pressures control* you and your future.

Which camp do you fall into? It's worth a moment of your time to think about it.

And just in case you're not sure, take a look at some of the signs that your purpose is not clear enough or strong enough—that you're living and working *off purpose* instead of *on purpose*. And take a look at some of the pressures that may have thrown your purpose into a long-forgotten memory. For each of the areas listed below, score yourself from 1 to 10, where one stands for the fact that "you feel none of those pressures" to 10 that means "you feel an intense amount of pressure in that area."

- *Career pressures*: You're not sure what your personal or professional goals are, and if you did know, you wouldn't know how to achieve them. You want to be engaged in meaningful work, in a growing career that you truly enjoy, but you're beginning to wonder if this is as far as you're ever going to go. You spend a lot of time thinking about what it might be like to start over or move "down" to a less responsible position that gives you more control of your life. You begin to think that "getting ahead" in life and work should mean more than simply "moving up" in the company. You wonder if it would make more sense to start your own business or do what you really love to do even though the pay may not be as good.

Your score _____

- *Job pressures*: You're willing to cancel some important personal time for a business issue of any kind. You lack time for yourself, time to read, relax, play, travel, or engage in a hobby. When you go out to dinner with your partner, you automatically answer any incoming phone call. You check your business voice mail when you're running errands over the weekend. And when you go on vacation you still stay in touch with the office. The thrill of closing a major deal isn't quite what it was a few years ago. You have a secure position, yet you're scanning the want ads and openings listed in professional journals. You have some health issues that you know are connected to your crazy work schedule.

Your score _____

- *Relational pressures*: You're not spending enough time with your partner or children. You know your work relationships could be stronger, but you don't have the time or the skills to improve those relationships. Your kids and partner are asking for more of your time, but you keep putting them off until later when you're not so busy.

Your score _____

- *Emotional pressures*: You're feeling increased stress, and your work and life seem to be getting more out of balance with each passing year. You're struggling to keep a positive attitude going all the time. You don't know how to grow spiritually and get the peace of mind you've always wanted. And there are times you feel like jumping ship and moving to some fantasy island. You find yourself thinking or saying, "What's the point? Why am I killing myself for this job?" You envy the guy who decides to follow his passion instead of his pocketbook. You are spending more time daydreaming about "the day I'll get out of this place." Or you just don't seem to have enough energy anymore.

Your score _____

How did you do? Your score could range from 4 to 40 points. If you have anything more than 20, please pay special attention to the chapters in this book on purpose. Because I have some great news for you. You don't have to stay put. You can get a well-defined, worthy purpose, which will in turn fire up the success of your career and life.

For the moment, however, if any of these pressures sound like you, if it hurts to admit that you're guilty of too many of these pressures, that's okay. It's even good, because the purpose of pain is to get your attention. Pain and pressure tell you that what you're doing isn't working all that well. And it's a good indication that you need to do some work on your purpose, because you know deep down something is missing.

At the beginning of this section I asked the question: Are you living by your priorities or your pressures? Some people get them all mixed up and pay a huge price as a result. I know. I fell into that trap.

I used to tell people that I may not be the smartest guy around, but I was by far the hardest worker. No one could outwork me. During my undergraduate college years, I always took the heaviest load of credits the university would allow, and I studied 25 hours for every final exam in every class, starting my studies weeks before the exams were given. On top of that I held a part-time job as a shoe salesman to make some extra money. Later, studying for my PhD exams, I would be in the library from 7:00 a.m. to midnight, seven days a week, for months on end, studying the entire time.

Later as a professor and then as a business owner, I used to wear my long hours of hard work or workaholic syndrome as a badge of honor. I'd say, "I go to bed at midnight, get up at 4:00 a.m. and then head off to my 60-hour workweek." I would even boast about my success, telling people that I got another promotion or was making more money than ever before.

All that hard work and pressure weren't necessarily bad things. One could even argue that those were good things. But it took my focus almost entirely off my higher priorities, such as my health, my marriage, my daughter, and my God. It took a painful, debilitating illness that temporarily robbed me of my ability to walk, and it took the loss of several key relationships before I realized I was tragically off base.

Today I know better. I even tease my workaholic students and audience members, telling them I hope to goodness they're successful, because all they do is work. It would be very embarrassing to be an unsuccessful workaholic.

With purpose, living and working your priorities, you have everything to gain and nothing to lose. With purpose, you will gain a lot: three payoffs in particular—better health, greater motivation, and deeper satisfaction.

Three Purpose Payoffs

The first huge payoff that comes from purpose is *vibrant health*, which may seem to be a strange thing to mention in a business book. But your physical health is too important to ignore.

Study after study connects purpose and lower disease rates, as well as greater longevity. For example, a study of 12,000 middle-aged Hungarians found that those who felt their lives had meaning had much lower rates of cancer and heart disease than those who didn't feel this way. Dr. Harold G. Koenig, a professor of psychiatry at Duke University Medical Center, says, "People who feel their life is part of a larger plan and are guided by their spiritual values have stronger immune systems, lower blood pressure, a lower risk of heart attack and cancer, and heal faster and live longer."[4] And Dan Buettner studied the world's longest living people and concluded that having a purpose or "having a reason to get out of bed" was a common trait among those people who lived past the age of 100.[5]

Your emotional health is similarly boosted by purpose. Noted educator Larry Wilson, author of *Play to Win: Choosing Growth over Fear in Work and Life* (Austin, TX: Bard Press, 1998), said, "Finding your purpose is the most emotionally healing thing you can do." When you're living on purpose, instead of by hit and by miss, you feel like your life and career count for something. And your emotional health is stronger as a result.

The second huge payoff that comes from purpose is *compelling motivation*. When you get a well-defined and worthy purpose, you get lasting motivation that doesn't wither away when difficulties get in your way at work or at home.

The right purpose makes you want to do something worthwhile. I learned that from my research on the Holocaust of World War II. I wondered how people made it through that horrible event in human history. So I visited such places as the concentration camps at Dachau and Auschwitz and Yad Vashem, the memorial to the Jewish victims of the Holocaust in Jerusalem, and I read numerous books on the subject.

The book that really caught my attention was *Man's Search for Meaning* (Boston, MA: Beacon Press, 1959) by Dr. Viktor Frankl. As a young Jewish psychiatrist, he was shipped off to Auschwitz. There in the worst of conditions, with little food, inadequate shelter, and horrendous torture, thousands of Jewish prisoners were forced into excruciating labor that went on for months.

What amazed Frankl was the fact that some of the laborers survived. While others, in the same conditions, did not. What Frankl found was that the ones who made it through those circumstances—and weren't sent to the gas chambers—had a compelling purpose. They had a purpose that said, "I will do whatever it takes to get out of this place, to find my wife, to find my kids, to reunite my family."

Frankl survived the war and lived into his nineties, writing and lecturing about the power of purpose. Frankl noted that Friedrich Nietzsche, the German philosopher (1844–1900), was right when he said, "He who has a 'why' to live for can bear almost any 'how.'"[6]

If you know your purpose, if you know "why" something is critically important to you, you can make it through almost anything. A compelling purpose gives you incredible motivation and endurance.

The third huge payoff that comes from purpose is *deeper satisfaction*. When I survey people and ask them what they want out of life, most of them say, "I just want to be happy." When I push them to explain what happiness means to them, they'll rattle off such things as a bigger house, a nicer car, finer clothes, or more exotic vacations. Their definition of happiness is connected to *things* in some way. But that seldom if ever brings happiness. A healthy, inspiring purpose is seldom connected to the pursuit of things, fame, or fortune.

Take it from Kevin Anderson, the author of *Divinity in Disguise* (Monclova, OH: Center for Life Balance, 2003). He writes, "Money and possessions are like diet soda—they satisfy momentarily, but they do not nourish." Or take it from Jim Carrey, the movie star. He says, "I believe everyone should become rich and successful so they can see that is not the answer."

The same goes for almost any spiritual philosophy you want to consult. You'll find them saying that a deep sense of satisfaction doesn't come from things, and it doesn't come with mere accomplishments. It comes from purpose. In particular a purpose connected to helping others in some way.

That's what the actor Kirk Douglas learned when he was 86 years old. After playing the strong, virile, tough guy in 82 films, he suffered a stroke, making him totally helpless for a while.

Then he found a new purpose, rebuilding school playgrounds that had become too old, dilapidated, or dangerous to use. He began raising money and even selling items from his personal art collection—including original paintings by Picasso and Van Gogh—to help schools with this project. He and his wife, Anne, went on to rebuild and appear at the reopening of hundreds of playgrounds[7] and, in the process, gained the satisfaction and meaning they were craving.

It's what the world-famous psychiatrist, Dr. Karl Menninger, stressed throughout his life. After giving a lecture on mental health, an audience member asked him, "What would you advise a person to do if that person felt a nervous breakdown coming on?"

Most people expected him to say, "Consult a psychiatrist." To their amazement, he replied, "Lock up your house. Go across the railway tracks. Find someone in need, and do something to help that person." In other words, when you stop thinking about your problems and start thinking about how you could help someone else, you'll have a purpose that will give you deep satisfaction.

If you're like me, all the stories, quotes, comments, experiences, and research studies in this chapter get me excited. I know, I absolutely know, that the power of purpose is the power that kicks *The Champion Edge* into start mode. So let's move on to what you need to do to discover, capture, and clarify your purpose.

CHAPTER 4

The Discovery of Purpose

Don't Confuse Your Job with Your Purpose

A few years ago, one of my mentees in the medical device industry asked me, "How and when did you know your life was going in the right direction?" And my floodgates opened and memory and emotion spilled out.

In junior high school, I had decided that I was going into the ministry, which to me meant I would end up being a pastor in a church. I hadn't given it too much thought or sought any other alternatives. It was simply the foregone conclusion of what I thought God and everybody else expected of me. My grandmother even offered to pay all my educational expenses, because it was her dream to have a pastor in the family. The problem was I wasn't sure it was my dream—or ever had been.

Nonetheless, I continued to prepare for my religious vocation as an undergraduate student by taking all the pre-theology classes: Greek, philosophy, and a host of other courses that did not excite me.

As my graduation from college came closer, I knew I didn't want to go to seminary, and I didn't want to become a pastor. It wasn't a matter of losing my faith; I just knew that I didn't want *that* particular job. And I had a dilemma. I was about to graduate and had no idea what I would do for a living. I had prepared myself for a job that I no longer wanted, somehow thinking that a *job* was my *purpose* in life.

To deal with my indecision, to give me time to think, to cover up my guilt, and to escape the seminary, I went on to get my master's and doctoral degrees, even though I had no particular desire to get those degrees and certainly no idea what I would do with those degrees once I got them. But I taught several undergraduate classes while I was pursuing my graduate education so I could pay for my tuition and expenses.

However, something strange happened. I discovered I loved teaching and I was good at it—very good, indeed. But I also felt guilty for tossing aside my "supposed" purpose or calling to the ministry.

After graduate school, and still confused about my purpose and career, I accepted a teaching position at Emporia Kansas State University, teaching interpersonal communication for business majors. It felt good when I was selected by the students as the "most outstanding professor" on campus, but I still felt guilty for not pursuing the religious job I had announced so many years before. Indeed, my feeling of uneasiness continued to grow. I was stuck between what I thought I should be doing and what I wanted to do.

Fortunately, in the midst of the struggle, I attended a weekend workshop on the process of "intensive journaling" taught by Dr. Ira Progoff. He taught me how to reflect, visualize, and keep a journal, so that the deeper things inside me might be revealed. It was a life-changing experience. I suddenly realized that there were many ways to serve my God and other people, not just one, like I had thought, in a church setting. So I wrote in my journal, "I *can* serve God and others as a teacher, speaker, author, and business owner." Almost instantly, my guilt disappeared, and a sense of peace, direction, and well-being settled over me. I knew I was living my life and working my career on purpose instead of by accident.

For years *I had confused a job with a purpose.* My years of confusion were gone now. I finally learned that I could help others or do "ministry" in any job. So it only made sense to choose a job that I really, Really wanted to do *and* one for which I had some aptitude. And here I am, decades later, loving the work I do, feeling thankful that I've been able to touch the lives of thousands of people, because my life and work have lined up with my purpose.

The lesson became so very clear to me and hopefully to you as well. The payoffs start to roll in when you know that your life and your work, someway, somehow, are lined up with your purpose—at least some of the time. So that raises a critical question.

How Can You Discover Your Purpose?

It all comes down to the three critical but deceptively simple questions (shown in Figure 4.1). The three legs represent the three questions that will help you discover, determine, or clarify your purpose, and the seat of the stool represents your purpose. In other words, the convergent answer

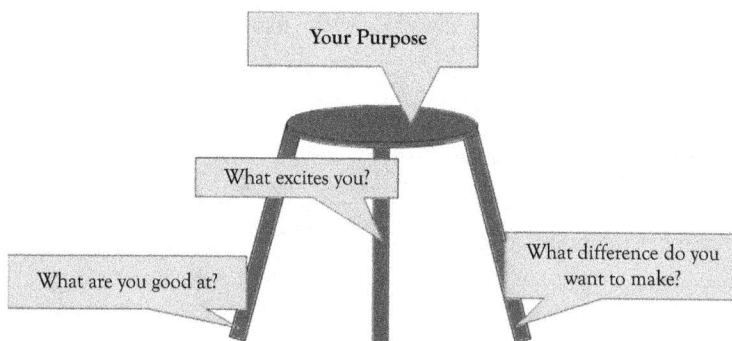

Your Purpose

What excites you?

What are you good at?

What difference do you want to make?

Figure 4.1 Three questions that reveal your purpose

to those three questions. Let's go through the three questions in some detail.

Question #1: What Are You Good At?

No matter who you are or what has happened in your life or career, you do have a lot of talents and abilities. You've got to know that. You may be gifted with numbers or work well with customers. You may be good at organizing projects or good at leading others. It's very difficult if not impossible to claim and use your strengths if you don't even know what they are.

So search your talents. Ask yourself some talent-clarifying questions. Take time to reflect on and write down your answers to questions such as these:

1. What are you good at?

   _____

2. What are your dominant gifts?

   _____

3. What natural abilities do you possess?

   _____

4. What tasks are easy for you to accomplish?

   _____

5. What do you do that gets a positive response from people you respect?

   _____

6. What do you do that does not seem like work, regardless of the difficulty?

_____

7. What do you do that causes doors to open with ease for you?

_____

You get the point. You have lots of things you're good at, whether or not you recognize those things. I want you to dig for those things and write out the longest list of talents you can possibly muster.

Tabulate your positive personal traits. A person could be highly talented, as the above questions might reveal, but still be a person you would never want to be around. Champions couple their talents with their traits. So start another list of all your positive personality traits. Perhaps you are gregarious, generous, organized, direct, confident, encouraging, creative, entrepreneurial, or a host of other things. Name and claim those traits that will eventually be used in your purpose.

_____

_____

Ask for input. In the process of writing, find out what others see as your talents. Don't dismiss their comments. If they keep asking you to do something, it's because they see your talent in that area. Ask them how they would describe you and your talents. Ask them to list the special skills and attributes you bring to every situation and interaction.

_____

_____

I'll even give you an assignment. Ask 15 people to each list 10 talents they see in you. Choose people from both your professional and personal lives. With your list of 150 items, determine which ones are repeated the most. Once you complete this exercise, you will be on your way to a clear picture of exactly what it is you're good at.

As you learn to clarify what you're good at, let me offer one caution. Do not dismiss *any* of your talents. Too many people say, "There's nothing special about me. I'm not particularly good at anything. I'm rather ordinary." That's not the way champions think or talk. So stop it!

A while ago, my wife, Chris, and I were hiking with our friends Mike and Jan Saarela in Glacier National Park. As luck would have it, we found a cafe on the edge of the park that advertised "Good, Old-Fashioned, Home Cooking."

When we finished our meal, the waitress said, "You really should try a piece of pie. My sister is the cook, and she bakes the *very* best pies you've ever tasted. In fact, we've got 23 different varieties."

So of course we had to try the pie. And it was terrific. I asked the waitress, "How did your sister become so good at making pies?"

In a few minutes, she returned with her sister, who had the happiest smile I had ever seen. It was obvious she enjoyed her work and took great satisfaction when her cooking was appreciated.

"Experience," she replied. "It's all in knowing how much of each ingredient to put in and baking it for just the right length of time. My father taught me, 'When you learn to do something right, and enjoy doing it, stick with it.' I love baking. And I love making people happy, so much so that I've been perfecting my pies for 18 years now."

"Well your pies are so good," we told her, "that we'll take one with us." I really hate to admit this, but her pies were SO-O-O-O good that we stopped by her cafe to buy another pie every day for the next seven days. We wanted to try some of her other flavors—and we had no problem consuming an entire pie each day.

That baker was a champion because she didn't dismiss her talents. She knew what she was good at and that contributed to her sense of purpose in life.

As consultant Faith Ralston says, "Focusing on talents is not a luxury. It's the key to thriving in today's economy. The old rules aren't working anymore. We can't wait around hoping others will recognize or reward us. To thrive, we've got to recognize our talents and connect them to business results."

That's the first question in your search for purpose—the first leg of our three-legged stool—*What are you good at?* Now we'll move on to the next question.

Question #2: What Excites You?

Take a look at how you're wired. What turns on your energy and what turns it off? Some activities and some causes make you feel alive while other things seem to kill off your spirit.

Tom Bloch discovered this when he resigned his position as the CEO of H&R Block, cofounded by his father Henry Bloch. He gave up running a $2 billion tax preparation firm to become a teacher at St. Francis Xavier Middle School in Kansas City, Missouri. His annual salary dropped to a mere $15,000 a year, a tiny fraction of what he had earned before. But Bloch knew that his hectic schedule as CEO had been interfering with his top priority—his wife and two children.

Tom said, "The hardest part was telling my father. But I didn't want to look back on my life and say, 'Gee, you had an opportunity to play a bigger role in your children's lives and didn't take it.'"[1]

What excites *you*? For some of you, that will be an easy question to answer. For others, it may be a challenging question to answer. So let me break that question into a series of smaller questions. I suspect one or more of these questions will unlock a whole series of insights as to what excites you.

What Are Your Dreams?

What did you dream of doing when you were a child? What were your dreams when you graduated from high school or college? What are your dreams today?

_____

_____

If you're not sure, just ask yourself two questions.

1. *What would you do if you knew you could not fail?*

_____

_____

2. *What would you do if no one would say "no"?*

_____

_____

Your answers will clarify your dreams and help you realize what excites you.

Now I realize a dream can be a little scary. That's why so many people quash their dreams before they ever see the light of day. They squelch their dreams with worrisome thoughts such as, "How will I support myself?" "How do I know if this new idea will work?" "What will my spouse think?" or "How will my kids feel about this crazy dream of mine?" It's only natural to be a bit afraid of the unknown, when the future seems fuzzy and vague.

But take comfort in this thought. Once you get a dream, and once you have *The Champion Edge* working for you, your chances of personal and business success increase dramatically.

What Stirs Your Passion?

What do you believe in? What makes life worth living? And what would you die for? You don't want to look back on your life and wish you had lived it differently. Ask yourself these passion questions. And take time to think about these questions and write out your answers:

1. *What are you passionate about?*

   _____

2. *What do you love spending time on?*

   _____

3. *What makes you feel alive?*

   _____

4. *What activities do you enjoy the most at work, at home, or in social situations?*

   _____

5. *Where would you like to spend more time?*

   _____

6. *What desires keep tugging at your heart?*

   _____

7. *What is motivating you in the times you are most productive?*

   _____

8. *What do you do that makes you feel good emotionally and spiritually?*

   _____

Of course, these passion questions may not sound very corporate. And much of my work is speaking to people in corporations. But don't be too hasty in dismissing these passion questions. When you get right down to it, any good empowerment program, emotional intelligence program, or customer service program is all about tapping into the passion of people. And champion leaders inspire followership in others because they have a passion for the business and those who work in it. Once you've answered those questions, it's time for another.

What Troubles Your Spirit?

The things that upset you are a good clue to your purpose in life. So ask yourself,

1. *What grieves your heart?*

2. *What infuriates you the most?*

Your answers to these questions may point out a problem you want to solve. And that problem, or those problems, will point to your purpose, or a part of your purpose.

Such was the case with one little girl. She stood sobbing near a small church from which she had been turned away because she was told it was too crowded. "I can't go to Sunday school," she sobbed to the pastor as he walked by.

Seeing her shabby, unkempt appearance, the pastor guessed the reason and, taking her by the hand, took her inside and found a place for her in the Sunday school class. The child was so happy they had found room for her, and she went to bed that night thinking of the children who were left out because there was no room.

Some two years later, this child lay dead in one of the poor tenement buildings of her city. Her parents called for the pastor who had befriended their daughter to handle the final arrangements.

As her little body was being moved, a crumpled red purse was uncovered. Inside they found $0.57 and a note, scribbled in childish handwriting, which read: "This is to help build the little church bigger so more children can go to Sunday school." For two years she had saved her money.

The pastor tearfully read the note to his parishioners and challenged them to raise enough money for a larger building.

But the story does not end there. A newspaper learned of the story and published it. A wealthy realtor read the story and offered to sell the church a parcel of land, worth thousands of dollars, for $0.57. Checks came in from far and wide. Within five years the little girl's gift had increased to $250,000—a huge sum at that time, around the year 1900. The little girl's purpose had paid large dividends.

When you are in the city of Philadelphia, look up Temple Baptist Church, with a seating capacity of 3,300. And be sure to visit Temple University, where thousands of students are educated. Have a look, too, at the Good Samaritan Hospital and at a Sunday school building that houses hundreds of children.

In one of the rooms you can see the picture of the little girl whose $0.57, whose purpose in life, made remarkable history.[2] And as often happens, when you're driven by a purpose, it often ignites a purpose in others. But there's one more aspect to this question of what excites you.

What Work Do You Love to Do?

What pumps you up on a professional level? What would you really like to do? What do you like to talk about and think about professionally? Write it down. As Jack Jia, founder and leader of the Musely online platform for skincare medical treatment, says, "If you refuse to do something you believe in, your mind will never leave you alone."[3]

One of my audience members, Juan, talked about that. Even though he was a successful insurance salesman (which is a necessary and noble profession), Juan said he always wanted to be a doctor in a third-world country. But the sales profession promised to give him a great deal more money in a much quicker fashion than pursuing a medical career overseas. So he'd been selling insurance for 30 years.

Juan admitted that he had dragged himself out of bed, five days a week, for 30 years, to do something he didn't care that much about. If he had done what he really wanted to do, if he had become a doctor, he may have made less money overseas, but he almost certainly would have been a happier and more successful human being.

That's why I teach people in my *Journey-to-the-Extraordinary* program that having something to live *on* is the *good* life, but having something to live *for* is the *better* life. So ask yourself, "What would you choose to do—even if no one was paying you to do it?"

Then look deeper. Look at all the income-producing work you've done over the years. And ask yourself which parts of that work you liked the most. Ask yourself, "What would you do if money wasn't an issue?"

In fact, you might try the money-makes-no-difference game. Imagine that every person on earth is paid $30 an hour for work regardless of the job he or she performs. If that were the case, what job would you choose to do? If you choose to be a tree cutter in the forest, you would be paid $30 an hour. If you decide to be a brain surgeon, you would still receive $30 an hour. What would you love to do if money was not involved? Write it down.

Once you've figured out your answers to the first question (what you're good at) and the second question (what excites you), you've got to ask yourself the third critical question.

Question #3: What Difference Do You Want to Make?

The first two questions are focused on *you*—your talents and your feelings. But the third question focuses on people or situations outside of you.

Of course, we live in an age where we're told to "Go for the gusto" and "Get all you can." But is that the real bottom line in life? Is that what really counts?

When Richard Leider, the author of *The Power of Purpose* (San Francisco, CA: Berrett-Koehler Publishers, 2010), interviewed scores of people over the age of 65, he asked them to share the most important lessons they had learned and what advice they would give younger people so they might have more fulfilling, successful lives and careers. Without hesitation, they said you've got to live a life that matters to others, and you've got to make a contribution to others. Go out there and make a difference in your world, whatever that might be, with whomever that might include.[4]

The good news is you don't have to wait until you're old before you learn how to live and what kind of career makes the most sense. You can get a purpose right now.

That's what Troyal learned. Troyal went to Oklahoma State University on a javelin-throwing scholarship, but athletics did not feel like his real calling. So he asked himself a crucial question: "If God came to earth with a box containing the reason for my life inside of it, what words would I most like to find in that box?"

It didn't take long for Troyal to know that the box would contain the word "music." He could pick a little guitar; his voice wasn't too bad, and he had written some songs. So he set off for Nashville.

Troyal did not find instant success in Nashville. He returned to Oklahoma, but two years later, he was back in Nashville working at a boot shop. One night he showed up for auditions at the Bluebird Cafe where a Columbia Records scout caught his act. The scout liked what he heard, offered a recording contract, and the rest is history.

Today this singer is known as Garth Brooks, the best-selling country artist of all time. According to PlanetGarth.com, he's sold more records than legendary Michael Jackson or Madonna. But it all started with purpose. When Garth Brooks realized his purpose had something to do with music, when he realized the difference he wanted to make was to bring a bit more joy to the world through his music, happiness and success followed.

What difference do you want to make with your career and your life? Think about it. And write it down.

The difference you want to make may not be as big as rescuing the poor of Calcutta like Mother Teresa. The difference you want to make may not gather worldwide headlines like Dr. Martin Luther King Jr.'s "I Have a Dream" speech.

That's okay. The difference *you* want to make may be in your immediate family, in your company, with your customers, or even some part of the world at large. But you must focus some part of your life and career on making a difference. Otherwise, you may have a good life, but you will never have a great life.

Put Your Answers into a Purpose Statement

Ultimately, you've got to have all three answers. You have to discover what you're good at. You have to figure out what excites you. And you have to know what difference you want to make. In the *convergence* of those three answers you will find your purpose.

Author and CEO Bob Buford writes, "If you look deeply enough inside of you and are honest about *combining* your competence with your passion, you will find the mission that is best suited to you."[5]

Notice my emphasis on the words *convergence* and *combining*. Your answers to the three questions I've just outlined will help you find and/or clarify your purpose.

Once you've figured out your answers, you need to write out your purpose statement. In its simplest form, your purpose statement is nothing more than one or two sentences that state why you are here and what you intend to do about it. It's a sentence or two that you live by, and it guides every one of your thoughts, actions, and decisions. It's like the steering wheel of your car or the guidance system installed in a rocket. So it's a really big deal.

Now don't let that scare you. Your purpose statement should be short and clear. It's simple. You don't need a thesaurus to write it. And you don't need a dictionary to understand it. A useful purpose makes instant sense. You know exactly what it says and what it means.

It gets right to the point. Take, for example, the purpose statements for several of my clients.

- 3M says: "Our purpose is to solve unsolved problems innovatively."
- Merck says: "Our purpose is to preserve and improve human life."
- Sony says: "Our purpose is to experience the joy of advancing and applying technology for the benefit of the public."

Their purpose statements tell you exactly why they are in business and what they plan to do. In fact, their purpose statements are so simple that any one of their thousands of employees could easily memorize and state their purpose, but, more important, they can do a quick "gut check" on whether the work they are doing is consistent with that purpose.

Still not sure what your purpose is or how to write it? Then try this. Write out a sentence that is structured like this.

- **"My purpose in life is to** _____ (insert an action verb . . . to do what?)
- **people who** _____ (specify the types of people to whom your purpose applies)
- **to** _____**."** (specify the difference you want to make in their lives)

One of the people who attended my *Journey to the Extraordinary* program, 31-year-old defense contractor Sheila wrote: "My purpose in life is to be a mom that helps her children become confident, self-reliant, effective individuals, partly by being a positive, supportive role model." And Bob, a tire manufacturing leader, wrote: "My business purpose is to show my employees and my customers that the best results come from honest, ethical, and caring behavior."

Of course, you may have more than one purpose statement. You might have one for your personal life and one for your professional life. No problem. While my personal purpose statement incorporates my family, faith, and community, my professional purpose statement says, "My purpose in business is to give my clients the skills and motivation they need to achieve their goals and build their relationships—on and off the job."

Once you've got your purpose statement or statements written out, congratulations! You're ahead of almost everybody else on this planet. You've got *The Champion Edge* off the ground and starting to work for you.

But there's one final issue we need to address. Some people do all the work to figure out a healthy, effective, and motivating purpose for themselves, but then they get off track. They live a life or perform work that is not in sync with their purpose. So how can you make sure you live your life and perform your work *on* purpose? Read on.

CHAPTER 5

The Practice of Purpose

Make Sure You Walk Your Talk

You've heard the old proverb that the road to hell is paved with good intentions. I'm not sure that's correct, but I do know that good intentions are never good enough. *The Champion Edge* is all about taking *action*. About walking your talk. As master artist Pablo Picasso declared, "What one does is what counts. Not what one had the intention of doing."

If you followed through on the last chapter, you now have a purpose statement. You've put your good intentions into writing. Congratulations! That puts you in *Champion Edge* territory, among the top tier of people. Because many psychologists and business consultants believe that only three percent of the population ever bothers to do that, and that three percent tends to be the highest achievers.[1]

Now you have to put your purpose into *practice.* The way I see it, you have two choices every morning: you can continue to sleep with your dreams or wake up and chase them. Champions always choose the second alternative. They walk their talk. They not only have a purpose statement with lots of good intentions, they follow through. As humorist Mark Twain said so very well, "Good intentions are like crying babies in church. They should be carried out immediately."[2]

The difficulty comes when the rubber hits the road. Your life and work can be busy, crazy, distracting, and overwhelming. And in the midst of all that, you can forget about your purpose. That's understandable but not smart. To stay *on purpose*, I've found the following practices to be invaluable. Read through them and *decide* which ones you're going to adopt, starting right now.

Purpose Practice #1: Listen to the Right People

Everybody has opinions. But just because somebody has opinions does not mean you should pay attention to them.

As entrepreneurial expert Dan S. Kennedy says, "The reason a lot of people never get ahead is they keep soliciting and paying attention to the opinions of the ignorant." He's so right.

Your brother, for example, may be a wonderful man, a good husband and father, and a great gardener, but that narrows the range of his opinions you ought to pay attention to—marriage, parenting, and gardening. That leaves out business growth, team building, and leadership development.

If you want to know how to fix your car, I'm the wrong guy to ask for advice. And I'm the wrong guy to take advice from—if I offer it. I hardly know the difference between a fan belt and a seat belt.

If you want to know how to build a positive attitude in yourself or your organization, or if you want to know how to motivate your team in times of change, I'm a great guy to get advice from. I've helped thousands of people do exactly that. Here are just two examples.

> Judi, a Senior Business Partner at the Target Corporation, testifies to that. She says, "We are being challenged to make changes we never thought possible. So your program on accepting change and keeping a positive attitude was right on target. I had many people take time to stop by my desk after the workshop to share with me their personal insight, and how they are putting into practice the principles you presented that day.

I also received many, many e-mail communications thanking me for arranging the session and telling me how useful it was."

Andy, the CEO of Medline, echoes that sentiment. He says, "As you know, we were concerned about our leadership meeting. *We weren't sure anyone could connect with our top leadership team and get them to change,* and the last thing we needed was a retreat that bombed. Our fears were quickly put to rest. *Our leaders soaked up everything you said, and you were able to thoroughly engage each and every one of them.* We couldn't be more pleased. Thank you for a great meeting. The feedback has been TREMENDOUS. Our paths must cross again … soon."

The point is people are quick to dispense advice on any subject, regardless of their qualifications to do so. It makes them feel important.

They rarely give any thought to their qualifications. They just spout out their opinions. They don't even distinguish between their opinions and true knowledge. That's why you must make sure you are listening to the right people.

As an author and professional speaker, I often help my clients create strategies that will make them more positive, productive, and profitable. But then those same clients are assaulted with ignorant opinion providers. Their spouse, their coworker, another department will gang up on them and harshly criticize the strategies we have created. They'll say, "That would never work." "It costs too much." Or "I just don't like the idea."

Unfortunately, none of those opinion givers has any real knowledge or expertise in business career development. None of them has spent 30 years of time and research on the topic like I have. As Dan S. Kennedy would say, "They have a constitutional right to their ignorant opinions, but you have an entrepreneurial responsibility to ignore them."

To stay on purpose, choose wisely the people to whom you will listen. And choose to ignore the negative opinions of the uninformed naysayers.

Purpose Practice #2: Start Your Day with a Six-Pack

We all have a million things we could put on our to-do lists. That's never a problem. The problem is how you spend your time on a daily basis. If you spend your time reacting or overreacting to things as they pop up, you've got a problem. If you allow distractions and interruptions to steal your focus, you've got a problem. And if you end up wondering where the day went or wondering why you never get anything done, you've got a problem. In every one of those cases, most of your day was spent *off purpose.*

To get away from those problems, get a six-pack. Identify the six most important things—or the six highest-value items—on your possible to-do list, and focus on those six things for the day. *Make sure that at least three or more of them have something to do with your purpose.*

Forget about those to-do lists that are longer than your arm. Remember, there are only 24 hours in a day. You can't get it all done, so focus on your six-pack.

Efficiency expert Ivy Ledbetter Lee (1877–1934) understood this when he pitched his consulting services to a steel mill that was struggling with profitability and survivability. He told the company's stone-faced president, Charles Schwab (1862–1939), "If you allow me the chance to help, I'll teach you and your executives to manage better. You'll know how . . ."

Schwab cut him off. "Look, Mr. Lee, I'm sure your services are great, but we don't need them. We don't need any more 'knowing' around here. I don't manage as well as I know how to now." He shook his head. "We already know what we should be doing. If you can show us a way to get it done better, I'll pay you anything you want."

Lee stepped toward the president's desk. "What if I could give you something in the next twenty minutes that would raise your efficiency by 50 percent?" Schwab raised an eyebrow and tilted his head slightly. "Go on."

Lee said, "Take a piece of paper and write down the six most important things you need to do tomorrow." Schwab thought for a couple of minutes and scribbled down six items. After he finished, he tossed his pen back onto the desk. "Now what?"

Lee folded his arms and looked down at the paper. "Now number them in order of importance." Schwab reached across the desk to grab the pen he had just flung. It only took a moment to put them in order. This time he laid the pen on top of the list. He gave a nod. "There."

Lee smiled.

Now, tomorrow when you get to work, I want you to work on the first item until it is done. Distractions will arise. Ignore them. Work on number one until it is done. Then move on to number two, then when that's all finished, number three, and so on. At the end of every day, make a new list. Don't worry about the things that don't get done. You will know you have been doing the most good possible for your company, and if you can't get all your items done using this method, you couldn't get them done using any other system either. Once you've had time to prove to yourself the value of this, have your people try it out as well. In fact, try it out as long as you like. Then, you send me a check for whatever you think it is worth.

The steel mill president stood up and extended a hand, but he looked lost in thought. Several weeks later, Lee received a letter in which Schwab informed him that his "list of six most important things" idea was the most profitable thing, from a money standpoint, that he had ever learned. Enclosed in the letter was a check for $25,000.[3]

How much will it be worth to you to stay on purpose?

Purpose Practice #3: Keep Your Six-Pack Visible

You know the old slogan "Out of sight, out of mind." It's so true when it comes to living your life on purpose. If you don't keep your six-pack clearly in view, you'll be tempted to work on other things and never get to your six-pack. You've got to keep your purpose in the forefront of your mind.

Try Jim Meisenheimer's method. He's one of the most effective sales trainers and time managers I've ever come across. When I visited his office, I noticed a two-foot by three-foot whiteboard mounted on an easel directly across from his desk. On the board, prominently displayed, were his six purpose-driven priorities for the day. It's no wonder he gets so much done; his purpose and his goal-related activities are staring him in the face all day long. And the same thing should be said about your purpose and supporting goals.

Purpose Practice #4: Ask a Clarifying Question

Even though people are constantly complaining about the lack of peace and quiet in their lives, they indiscriminately give away what little peace and quiet they still have left. They give away their cell phone numbers to just about any Tom, Dick, and Harry "just in case you need to get a hold of me." Even though Meisenheimer is in sales, he says that's crazy, "You may as well go to a tattoo parlor and get 24/7 printed on your forehead when you give everybody your cell number."

Even if you have your written purpose within eyesight much of the day, you're still going to be tempted to stray off task. You're going to be confronted with dozens of supposedly urgent crises that need to be handled immediately.

When that happens, pause. Catch your breath. Call time out. Disconnect from the frenzy. Don't allow yourself to be caught in the rip-tide. Stop running and take time to pause and reflect on your purpose. Clarify what's really important. Ask yourself: *Will this action bring me closer to my purpose or take me further away from it?*

Purpose Practice #5: Engage in Purpose-Fulfilling Activity Every Day

I learned that lesson years ago. For years, I kept saying my kids were important to me. They were a part of my purpose in life. That was my *talk*.

But my *walk* was quite different. I was out speaking to groups, all the time, across the world and was seldom home. I missed most of my kids' events. But I rationalized my behavior. I was important; I was in demand; I had to work to pay the bills, and I had a professional purpose that overshadowed—or should I say, "blotted out"—any personal purpose I claimed to have.

But there came a time when I realized I could no longer say one thing—and do another—and feel good about myself. I could no longer say my kids were important to me and continue to miss out on so much of their lives. If I was going to be a man who lived his life on purpose, a man who walked his talk, if I was going to be a man of integrity, I would have to cut back on my travel schedule so I could spend more time with my kids. And I did.

So I ask you, "Are there any gaps between your talk and your walk? And do you need to make any changes in your life or in your career to close those gaps?"

There is simply no way you can have self-esteem, integrity, or peace of mind if you profess one set of values but live another. And there is simply no way you can be at your best and produce your best if you're not living your life *on* purpose and engaging in some purpose-fulfilling activity *every day*.

After attending one of my seminars, bank executive Jill did exactly that. She got a purpose of creating a more positive family environment and went to work on it—*every day*. She wrote me the following note:

There was such a spirit of negativity and ungratefulness in my home that I knew I had to do something different or else die trying. I decided to start a journal with my children. Each night I asked each one of my kids to spend two minutes with me and fill out a piece of paper that had a few questions on it. I asked them to list: (1) at least one thing they were good at or liked doing, (2) one thing that they did to help someone else that day, (3) how it made them or the other person feel when they gave the help, and (4) one thing they were grateful for. I also asked them to pick a family member and jot down one strength or one good thing about that person *every day.*

Notice how Jill not only defined her purpose but she worked on her purpose *every day.* It was a critical part of the success she experienced. As Jill put it,

It was amazing what happened. After a few weeks, all of us were seeing opportunities to help others that we hadn't seen before. Helping others blessed others, brightened our day, and made us feel good. Self-esteem skyrocketed because my children were seeing and affirming the goodness in themselves and others. The contention in our home lessened, and we had more peace and happiness in our home and in our lives. Of course, my children found it hard at first to even admit that their siblings possessed any good qualities, but each one of my children has asked me to revisit the answers and tell them the good things their brothers or sisters have said about them. They loved it, even though they didn't want to participate at first.

In a sense, Jill's family learned what author Johnetta B. Cole taught. In her words, "While it is true that without a vision the people perish, it is doubly true that without action the people and their vision perish as well."[4]

With Your Purpose in Place . . .

Purpose is where *The Champion Edge* starts. Not just in sports but in all of life and business.

As Thomas Oppong, founder of Alltopstartups notes, "Defining your direction as early as possible is the most important decision in sports. But, curiously enough, this is also the most important decision in life in general, but much fewer people realize it."[5]

Well, *you* realize it. To get your purpose off your paper and working for you, it's time to unleash the second element of *The Champion Edge.* It's time to apply *passion* to your *purpose.*

PART II

Passion

CHAPTER 6

The Power of Passion

Where *The Champion Edge* Gets Fired Up

Purpose is the first skill set in *The Champion Edge*. And it is, without question, critically important. But purpose is only the first skill set. In and of itself, it will never bring you the payoffs you want, need, crave, and desire. You also need the power of *passion* working for you.

John Mahoney learned that. He had a purpose—helping others with the English language. But somewhere along the way he lost his passion. "When I was thirty-seven," Mahoney recalls, "I had gone through a career as an English teacher and a medical editor. But I was very dissatisfied with my life. So I thought, 'What did I ever do that brought me real joy?' Immediately I knew the answer. It was when I was acting. I thought, 'I've got to give it a try so at least I can say that I tried.'"[1]

He did. He reclaimed his passion, and it was at that point that Mahoney began a successful stage and film career as an actor. And chances are you know him for his portrayal of the father in the hit sitcom *Frasier*.

The power of *passion*! Sounds kind of sexy, doesn't it? It conjures up images of zeal, fervor, spirit, energy, romance, and excitement. It makes you think of a person who is all fired up. And it's true; passion has all those emotionally intelligent nuances.

But passion is so much more than that. Passion is not some nice-to-have soft skill without any bottom-line significance. Early in his career, author and business consultant Price Pritchett had a mentor who was a very skilled management psychologist. Time and again, Pritchett heard him say, "In my opinion, the single most important factor for success in the business world is a high energy level."

From the mentor's point of view, energy—or *passion*, as I'm calling it—contributed more to career success than having the right amount of intelligence, personality, and social skills. Passion contributed more to career success than getting certain advanced degrees, internships, or company affiliations. And after 25 years of consulting, Pritchett now says, "I can't guarantee that energy level is absolutely the single most important factor for career success. But I have become convinced it belongs in that small handful of most critical factors."[2]

Business adviser and author Mark C. Thompson concurs. After he interviewed dozens of corporate and government leaders around the world, Thompson concluded there's one distinguishing characteristic of successful leaders everywhere. He said, "It is *passion that makes the difference*. Being passionate about work transforms the best in us."

In fact, I consider my passion or energy level to be one of the secrets to my success. Anyone who knows me will comment on my energy level. I am filled with it almost all the time. I pack a lot into every day, and I live life to the fullest. It's the power of passion working in me.

And yet, I realize that lots of people do not have the passion or energy they need for greater success at work or at home. Maybe you're one of them. Maybe you're wondering, "What exactly goes into this passion thing? How do you get all fired up and keep that fire going?" That's what *passion* or part II, of *The Champion Edge* is all about. There's little need to know what your *purpose* is, the material I discussed in Part I, if you don't have the energy to do anything about it.

I've learned that good, healthy, lasting, abundant, and effective passion has three components. Let me give you a brief overview before we dig into the upcoming chapters.

Three Ingredients of Fired-Up Passion

For a fire to burn—and produce meaningful payoffs—it needs *fuel*, something like wood, oil, or coal. It needs *oxygen* or it gets choked out. And it needs *guidance*, something like a fire ring or a fireplace, or it can go in the wrong direction or even cause harm (see Figure 6.1).

Attitude, the Fuel

The first ingredient is *attitude*, which is similar to the fuel needed by a fire. Written some five thousand years ago, Proverbs 26:20 says, "Fire goes out for the lack of fuel."[3] And passion goes away without attitude.

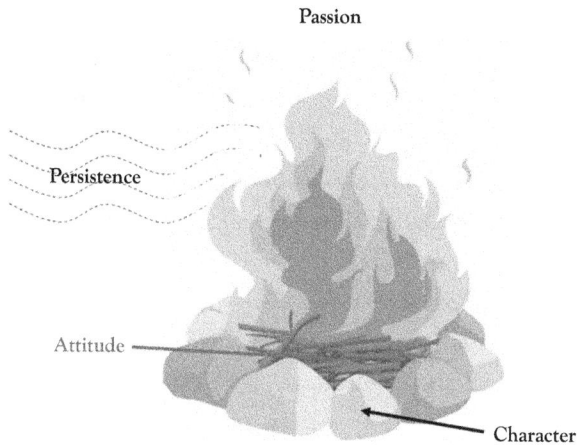

Figure 6.1 Three fired-up passion components

The more attitude you have—positive attitude, that is—the longer your fire will burn. Elizabeth Edwards spoke eloquently about this. Despite the fact that she was the wife of a presidential candidate, despite the fact that her husband betrayed her with a lover and a secret love child, and despite the fact that she was battling cancer, she said, "A positive attitude is not going to save you. What it's going to do is, every day, between now and the day you die, [is guarantee] that every day you're going to actually live."[4]

Entrepreneur Rachel Elnaugh added a business twist to Edwards' comment. Elnaugh said, "I would say that success is much more about a state of mind and an attitude than any sort of business skill. It's about keeping positive."

Persistence, the Oxygen

The second ingredient of passion is *persistence*, which is like the oxygen needed by a fire to keep on burning. Unfortunately, too many people let their fires get strangled. You hear it in their words when they say, "If only I would have . . ." "I wish I had . . ." "I should have . . ." and "Why didn't I . . .?"

Persistence is absolutely essential if you're going to get the payoffs you want. As President Calvin Coolidge noted, "Nothing in the world can take the place of persistence. Talent will not; nothing is more common than unsuccessful men with talent. Genius will not; unrewarded genius is almost a proverb. Education will not; the world is full of educated derelicts. Persistence and determination alone are omnipotent."[5]

He was absolutely correct. When you read about persistence in an upcoming chapter, you'll learn exactly what you have to do to keep on keeping on whether you feel like it or not.

Now this is where almost every business, career, success, self-help, and motivation book stop. They try to get you fired up with attitude and persistence and leave it at that. But that's dangerous. As I tell my audiences, "If you motivate an idiot, all you get is a motivated idiot." And our society already has too many gruesome, exasperating examples of that.

To make sure your fired-up passion works for you instead of against you, to make sure your fire doesn't make you act like some motivated idiot, you need to guide your fire. As you know, if you don't guide a fire, it can consume a home, a business, a neighborhood, a relationship, and everyone inside.

Character, the Fire Ring

I refer to that needed guidance as *character*. And character is the third ingredient of passion, serving as a fire ring to make sure your fire burns smart. Unfortunately, I had to learn about character in an embarrassing way. I had lots of attitude and lots of persistence, but I didn't always have the character I needed to guide the use of my passion.

For example, I never played sports in high school. I could tell you that I had no interest in sports, which was partially true, because I was much more interested in debate, theater, radio, television, and competitive speaking. But the deeper truth was, even if I did have an interest, I would never have been chosen to be on one of the teams. I was too fat, slow, and awkward.

However, I was selected to announce the basketball games at my high school for three years. I knew something about the game, rather enjoyed it, and was able to use my speaking talents. I felt pretty good about myself. I figured if I couldn't be "on the court," I could at least be "on the air." It gave me a bit of recognition and a bit of a big head. But it didn't take too long to realize that my big-headed passion was missing the guiding element of character.

When I entered college, I was immediately asked to be the sports announcer for my University of Wisconsin football team. My reaction was, "Yeah. Wow. A bigger crowd, a bigger arena, more recognition, and more prestige." I had passion, to be sure, but I was also a motivated idiot.

It wasn't until after I accepted the job as the football announcer that I realized I knew nothing about football. Absolutely nothing! I didn't know any of the rules, moves, plays, or anything else.

As the first football game approached, the game I was to announce, panic set in. How could I possibly announce the game? I asked my brother David, who played football throughout his high school years, to come to the game with me. Together we sat high above the stadium, where the sports announcers sit, and my brother would tell me what was happening in the game. He literally told me what to say, and I repeated it over the public address (PA) system and the radio. I don't know how many people in the stands noticed the delay between what was happening in the game and my comments on it. But I knew my performance was lackluster at best, and I knew the people deserved better. I resigned the announcer's job after the first game.

Sure, I had two of the three components of passion. I had a positive attitude toward the job, and I had the persistence to pursue the job. But I lacked the character component to guide that passion and tell me that I wasn't the best person for the job. I needed all three components, and so do you.

CHAPTER 7

The Attitude of Passion

Attitude: The Fuel Supply for Your Fire

When you have a positive attitude as the fuel for your fire and passion, you have more of *The Champion Edge* working for you, and your payoffs are huge.

For example, in the early 1900s, one of the pioneers of modern-day psychology Dr. William James (Harvard University even named a building after him) proclaimed, "It is our attitude at the beginning of a difficult task which, *more than anything else*, will affect its successful outcome."

Around that same time, French literary theorist Tom Blandi wrote, "Our attitudes *control* our lives. Attitudes are a secret power working twenty-four hours a day, for good or bad. It is of paramount importance that we know how to harness and control this great force."[1]

The father of positive thinking, Dr. Norman Vincent Peale (1898–1993) declared, "There is a basic law that like attracts like. Negative thinking definitely attracts negative results. Conversely, if a person habitually thinks optimistically and hopefully, his positive thinking sets in motion creative forces, and success . . . instead of eluding him . . . flows toward him." In plain terms, good attitudes attract good results and bad attitudes attract bad results. It's that simple.

And the most recent research from Jon Gordon, the author/speaker, goes a step further. He writes, "The research is clear. It *really does pay* to be positive . . . Being positive is not just a nice way to live. It's *the* way to live."[2]

Of course, cynical non-champions may respond by saying, "Oh yeah. Really? What's in it for me?" Actually you can expect several major payoffs in your business career and life if your attitudes don't stink.

The Attitude Payoff

To those of you are skeptical of the "soft-skill science" of attitude, mindset, or positive thinking, let me suggest a few of the payoffs you can expect with the right attitude. Of course, I could write a whole book to the subject, which I have already done, *Pivot: How One Turn in Attitude Can Lead to Success* (Peak Performance Publications, 2006). But here are two payoffs for starters.

1. **Higher income in your career**

   Numerous studies indicate that positive leaders and positive team members behave in ways in which they create—or receive—more pay raises and more promotions than those with a negative attitude.

   In one particularly fascinating study, Dr. Martin Seligman reported on 1,500 people. Group A (or 83 percent of the people) chose their jobs because they believed they could make a lot of money. Group B (only 17 percent) chose their jobs because they had a positive attitude toward the job.

   Twenty years later, Seligman noted the two groups had produced 101 millionaires. But only one millionaire came from group A (people who chose a particular job to make a lot of money). The other 100 millionaires came from group B (people who chose their jobs because of a positive attitude toward the job). Attitude had made a huge difference in their eventual incomes.

   Speaking more broadly, Seligman even noted that salespeople fueled by a positive attitude sell more, and make more money, than pessimistic salespeople. Well, of course. Who wants to buy anything from a grouch? And that only makes sense because positive attitudes lead to positive behaviors, which lead to more productive work relationships.

2. **More opportunities for advancement**

   That's partly because a good attitude helps you *see* opportunities you would have missed with a more negative attitude. Earl Nightingale, the 20th century's foremost authority on success, said, "A great attitude does much more than turn on the lights in our worlds. It seems to magically connect us to all sorts of serendipitous opportunities that were somehow absent before we changed."[3]

   For example, the person with a negative attitude thinks, "It's never been done before." A champion sees an opportunity and says, "We have the chance to be first." The negative thinker says, "It's good enough." While the champion sees it differently and says, "There's always room for improvement."

Presuming you understand the importance of attitude in your pursuit of *The Champion Edge*, let me suggest that you first need to determine the current state of your attitude. And then second, build it up, if necessary.

How Positive and Powerful is Your Attitude?

Take a look at your attitudes to see how well they are serving you. Are you more positive or more negative? There are four tests you can take to get an answer to that question.

Test #1: Survey Some People Who Know You

Ask 10 of your closest friends and family members if they would rate you as "more positive" or "more negative." Ask the same question of another 10 people at work. If you get more than seven of the 20 people saying you're "more negative," it's time for you to fuel up your attitude. You're too negative for your own good.

Test #2: Check Out Your First Reaction to Any Bit of News You Get

If, for example, you get e-mail from your boss that says, "See me immediately," what is your first reaction? Is your first reaction, "Great, the raise is coming early this year"? Or is your first reaction, "What did I do wrong this time"? Eighty-five percent of people expect the negative and, therefore, are more negatively programmed.

Test #3: Observe Your Daily Comments

See if you can go 24 hours without uttering one single negative comment. That's right; see if you can go 24 hours without making any negative remarks about the weather, your workload, a particular customer, a family member, an item in the news, or anything else.

You may be addicted to negative thinking and negative talking without even knowing about it. If, for example, you can't go 24 hours without a cigarette, you're addicted to nicotine. If you can't go 24 hours without an alcoholic drink, you're addicted to alcohol. And the same principle applies to your communication. If you can't go 24 hours without complaining about something, worrying about someone, griping about something, or putting someone down, you're addicted to the negative. You need to fire up your attitude.

Test #4: See How You Stack Up against a Checklist

People with a positive attitude, exhibit some fairly consistent behavior patterns. Inspired by author Craig Jarrow,[4] I developed the following checklist. Go ahead and circle each item that describes you, most of the time:

- Smiling and laughing frequently.
- Being happy for someone else's success.
- Giving more than you expect to get in return.
- Having a good time even when you are losing.
- Not getting what you want and not pitching a fit.
- Always have an uplifting word to share with others.
- Refusing to let other people's negativity bring you down.
- Getting back up no matter how many times you fall down.
- Understanding that people are more important than things.
- Being happy even when you have very little to be happy about.
- Refusing to complain, no matter how unfair things appear to be.
- Expecting good things to happen, even if your present situation is difficult.

If you circled seven or more of these behaviors, you tend to fall on the positive side.

Based on the four tests you've just taken, how positive and powerful is your attitude? Is it everything it needs to be? Is it serving you well? Is it advancing your life and career or is it holding you back? Most people conclude that their attitude needs to be more positive and more powerful if they're going to be a champion.

You Can Change Your Attitude

For a long time, one of my pet peeves was hearing people say, "I can't help the way I feel . . ." "That's just the way I am . . ." "I've always been that way . . ." or "I can't change." I thought they were wasting their lives. They were missing out on so many of the good things in life because they were saddled with a negative, self-limiting attitude.

Well, I no longer feel peeved by those people. I'm actually saddened by their comments. I now realize they're simply ignorant. They either *do not think it is possible* to change their attitude *or do not know how* to change their attitude.

With regard to their first point, I defer to Dr. William James, the prolific author, researcher, and Harvard professor, who wrote *"The greatest discovery of any generation is that a human can alter his life by altering his attitude."*[5] In other words, you absolutely *can* change your attitude.

With regard to the second point, that some people don't know how to change their attitude, here are seven ways you can do that.

Attitude Practice #1: Decide to Have a Positive Attitude

The Champion Edge starts *inside your head*—with purpose, as we discussed in previous chapters. And *The Champion Edge* continues to grow in strength and momentum *inside your head*, as you fire it up with the positive attitude that *you decide to have*.

Unfortunately, non-champions think a good attitude comes from the outside. They think their happiness is dependent on certain things happening in their lives, such as a raise in pay or the acquisition of a customer. But if other things happen, such as a drop in the stock market or a conflict with their spouse, they're unhappy.

That is a lousy, uninformed way to live. If you wait for a good attitude to suddenly appear in your arsenal of business success tools, if you wait for certain things to happen before you move forward emotionally or occupationally, you may wait forever. And you become the victim of circumstances, rather than the creator of them. You have to decide to have a positive attitude, no matter what, period!

I can already hear the skeptics saying, "Yeah, Dr. Zimmerman, that's easy for you to say. Just decide to have a positive attitude. You couldn't possibly understand how difficult my boss, job, coworkers, customers, finances, parents, spouse, or children are."

Wait a minute. I do understand. Firing up a positive attitude didn't come easily for me. I've come through a debilitating illness, divorce, and financial strain. I've seen my loved ones affected by abuse, alcoholism, imprisonment, and suicide. And I've encountered betrayal from coworkers, incompetent direction from bosses, and idiotic change from the executives above. Nonetheless, I decided to have a positive attitude, and that more than anything else kept me going and still does.

You may feel like the 30-year-old woman who wrote in her diary: "My God, what will become of me? I have no desire but to die. There's not a night that I do not lie down on my bed wishing that I may leave it no more. Unconsciousness is all that I desire."[6]

This woman's depression was overwhelming. Yet I would be willing to bet that you would never guess who wrote those words.

In fact, you might be quite surprised to learn that when she died 60 years later, she was said to be one of three people in the world who did the most to alleviate suffering in the 19th century. Her name was Florence Nightingale, the founder of the modern nursing profession.

When Florence *decided to have a positive attitude*—instead of wallowing in her negativity—her world, indeed the entire world, turned around. She learned that even though she had to go through seasons of pain, it was still possible to make significant gains in life.

The same is true for you. You can make a lot of progress in life. You can achieve major payoffs, even if life throws you a few curve balls, if you *decide* to have a positive attitude.

Attitude Practice #2: Feed Your Mind a Steady Diet of Positive Inputs

Yes, *feed*. You would never think of putting yourself on an all-candy diet if you were training for a marathon. You know that the fuel you put in your body, to a great extent, will determine your performance. You would feed your body the best foods you could get.

And yet, when it comes to feeding your mind for the life or career marathon you're on, most people disregard this basic piece of wisdom. They unconsciously let negative garbage into their minds, and they consciously do little or nothing to feed their mind the positive thoughts it needs.

I know. I was one of the guilty ones. For many years, my morning ritual began with a scan through some social media news outlets and then listening to the radio news as I drove to the office. After filling my mind with the day's murders, rapes, indictments, invasions, and all the other bad news, it shouldn't have come as a surprise that my attitude was less than positive.

I gave up this stupid morning ritual many years ago and replaced it with a steady diet of positive inputs. And it paid off in every part of my life. So, I highly recommend the following procedure.

Spend Five Minutes Every Day Thinking about Good Things

Think about good things in your job, your life, your family, the world around you, or whatever. It's what the Apostle Paul recommended about 2,000 years ago when he wrote, "Fix your thoughts on what is true and good and right. Think about things that are pure and lovely, and dwell on the fine, good things in others. Think about all you can praise God for and be glad about."[7]

Spend 10 Minutes Every Day Reading for Inspiration

Read things that will make you a better person and a better professional. And sorry, but Facebook, Instagram, and novels don't count when it comes to fueling your passion. Oh, you may learn something from those sources, and you should enjoy a good fiction read once in a while, but they will seldom do anything to help you build and maintain a positive attitude.

The most passionate people—the champions at work and in life—don't depend on yesterday's motivation for today's challenges. They spend at least 10 minutes a day putting positive, inspiring information into their minds.

Practice Word Therapy

Say such words as *indomitable, unsinkable, undefeatable,* and *victorious* throughout your day. Say them out loud if possible. And if you're going through an especially tough time, or if your attitude has been too negative for too long, add a bit of discipline to your word therapy. Instead of merely verbalizing these strong, self-empowering words once in a while, speak them three times a day, every day, for the next 30 days.

Surround Yourself with Positive People

Seek the company of upbeat, optimistic people. Eat lunch with coworkers who are more positive if your present luncheon companions are constant gripers. Surround yourself with nurturing people who build you up, believe in you, and encourage you. Attitudes are contagious; so make sure you're around people whose attitudes are worth catching.

Attitude Practice #3: Keep a Motivation Journal

Instead of keeping a diary of your days, keep a journal. Use it to write down all the good "stuff" you see, hear, find, learn, or experience. In your journal, record great ideas, inspiring quotes, key insights, important lessons, key phrases, what worked and didn't work, and all kinds of daily observations that are worth remembering.

In fact, have some fun with your journal. Write down the humorous lines you hear or read. They'll give you a laugh, and the laugh will add to your overall positive attitude. For example, I came across the following line and put it my journal: "The evening news is where they begin by saying 'Good evening' and then proceed to tell you why it isn't."

At the end of each day, before you retire, think of three or more good things that happened during your day. Write them down. And take a moment to reflect on why those good things occurred.

You get the idea. Keep a journal of the positive. And go back and read what you wrote once in a while. You'll be amazed at the wisdom you accumulate and the high it will give you.

Attitude Practice #4: Practice an Attitude of Gratitude

There's an old song that says, "Count your blessings, one by one." Evidently that advice was not only theologically correct but scientifically correct as well. Research shows that when you count three or more blessings a day, you get a measurable boost in your energy, your spirit, and your overall happiness. There are two ways you can do that.

1. **Be thankful for what you have.**

   Don't wait for a crisis to be reminded of what you have. And don't wait for the tough times to practice an attitude of gratitude.

   Lisa, one of my students who came from the agribusiness sector of the economy, reminded me of that when Hurricane Katrina destroyed her home. They had to evacuate to her sister's place in Atlanta. While there, her young nephew asked her if she got all the important things out of the house before she left. Lisa said, "While my mind raced through thoughts of important papers and photos and jewelry and sentimental items, my sister was quicker to respond to him than I was. She simply said, 'Yes, she got her husband and her children!'"

   To get yourself started, take two minutes to list all the things you're thankful for. And take another two minutes every day after that to list some more things for which you're thankful.

2. **Be thankful for what you don't have.**

   Personally, I like the way one anonymously written poem puts it. It says, in part, "Be thankful that you don't already have everything you desire. If you did, what would there be to look forward to? Be thankful when you don't know something, for it gives you the opportunity to learn."

Attitude Practice #5: Choose a Perspective That Serves You

People tend to think their way of seeing something is the *only* way to see it. Not so. There's *always* more than one way to see something, and the perspective you choose will make all the difference in your professional success and personal happiness.

I see it happen all the time in the workplace, where two people with the same job take different perspectives and, as a result, they get very different results. Salesperson A constantly complains that his company's prices are too high; his supporting sales materials aren't up to date; he doesn't have the latest software on his computer; his territory is too small; there are too few good prospects, and his support staff is inadequate.

Salesperson B has the same set of challenges. Instead of whining about it, he concludes he'd better spend more time than ever making face-to-face contact with his prospects and customers. He knows the success of his sales will depend, to a large degree, on the quality of the relationships he builds.

Given those two perspectives, guess who has the better track record in sales?

The truth is some perspectives invigorate you while others depress you. So ask yourself, "How well is my perspective *serving* me?" Does your perspective help you accomplish more? And feel better? Does your perspective give you lift and motivation? Or does it drag you down and hold you back? If your perspective is *not* serving you or is *not* making your life better, then you need to change it.

Choose a perspective that serves you well when difficulties come. Learn to be like the woman who said to her husband, "Our vacation is not a total loss, dear. Most people go an entire lifetime without ever seeing icicles on palm trees."

Attitude Practice #6: Act As If You Are Positive

Suppose there was a magic pill that gives you more energy, makes you less stressed, gives you more confidence, and makes you more productive. You'd probably take that pill, just like I would. In fact, you'd probably want a lifetime supply.

Well, the good news is there is such a pill on the market right now. And you don't have to go to a doctor, get a prescription, or worry about any side effects. The pill is found in what I call "the three most powerful words in the English language." All you have to do is *act as if*.

In the mid-20th century, the world-famous personal development specialist Dale Carnegie (1888–1955) commented on those three words.

He wrote, "Act as if you were already happy, and that will tend to make you happy."[8]

If you're wondering if this really works, look at Dr. Dale Anderson's research in the early 21st century. Anderson studied actors and actresses and discovered an amazing thing. When the actors and actresses played the role of a happy character, their internal chemistry changed dramatically. They not only felt better but their bodies exhibited all the signs of a healthier person.[9]

As a medical doctor, Anderson gave his patients a simple prescription: "Act positively." Act as if you're enthusiastic. Jump. Smile. Put an extra skip into your step. Add a lilt to your laugh. Fake it until you make it. And it doesn't matter what is happening in your life or how you feel—just act positively, and you will, without a doubt, feel better. And if you act positively, you will become more positive and passionate in your attitude.

Attitude Practice #7: Deflect the Negative

In the natural world, the law of gravity says what goes up must come down. In the psychological world, the law of exposure says what goes in must come out. If you're exposed to a lot of negatives, if you allow those negatives to *get into* your mind, they will *come out* in a more negative attitude.

The good news is you can choose which negative inputs will stay put. As entrepreneurship consultant Gladys Edmunds says, "Picture your thoughts as people passing by the front of your home. Just because they're walking by doesn't mean you have to invite them in."[10]

And in a similar sense, just because you're exposed to a barrage of negative news or negative people doesn't mean you have to let them in. You can let them pass on by. It will do wonders for your attitude. Try these strategies for deflecting the negative.

Limit Your Exposure to Negative Information

Obviously, you want to be informed about what is happening in the world, in the country, in your company, and in your family. You want to know enough so you can make the best judgments as to what you should do.

But once you know the news, shut it off. Cut back on the time you spend on the news, because overexposure to negative input has no redeeming value. It will not make your life better, help you sleep more soundly, make you more money, or improve your relationships. Negative input will only depress you. After all, the news now—like the news five, ten, or fifty years ago—is almost always negative and almost always repeated.

Limit Your Contact Time with Negative People

Your mama was right. Be careful about who you hang around with. If you spend too much time with negative people, it will be very difficult for you to stay fired up.

Perhaps you've noticed some folks at work talking on and on about how bad the economy is. Or you've heard some coworkers express their anger over the changes in the company. Be careful of spending too much time with gripers and complainers or moaners and groaners. If you're not careful, they'll drag you into their pit of despair. Or they'll suck you into the discussion, where you may start adding your own comments about how rotten everything is. And as you do, you'll kill off your own positive attitude, and you'll end up feeling worse than you did before.

Of course, some of you will protest, "I can't limit my contact time with some of the negative people in my life. That includes my spouse or boss, and I've got to be around them." If that's the case for you, then practice taking their negativity with a grain of salt or a healthy dose of skepticism. You can't let somebody else's negativity kill off your energy. You could even take it a step further.

Challenge the Negativity of Others

Challenging other's negativity may stop, or at least diminish, the other person's negativity so you don't have to hear so much of it in the future.

Personally, I like the way one of my small-business clients Reggie dealt with it. He told me he had a small office filled with employees who talked behind one another's backs and who were continually whining. He got so sick and tired of babysitting or policing them that he put up a complaint jar. Reggie said, "Whenever an employee would complain about an office policy, another employee, or anything else, they had to follow up with a constructive solution. If not, they had to put a quarter in the jar. I let the employees police themselves, and it cut way down on the petty complaints. Then we used the money for pizza and drinks at the next staff meeting."

Another one of my clients, Tracey from one of the largest federal agencies has a great way of challenging negative people as well. She says, "When people tell me how bad their day was, I tell them, 'If that is the worst thing that happened today, it must have been a pretty good day!' Amazing how that makes people stop and think."

There you have it, seven practices for building and keeping a fueled up, fired up, passionate, positive attitude. But you may still be wondering if a positive attitude *really* works. The answer is yes!

Positive Attitudes Always Work

That statement always raises a few eyebrows. In fact, a lot of people tell me, "I tried to adopt a more positive attitude, but it didn't work."

Oh really? Then I suspect you've got a messed-up definition as to what a positive attitude is and how it works. I know I struggled with the definition for several years. For a while, I thought that a person with a positive attitude would always be happy. Then I realized that was nonsense. It's not possible to live your life having only one emotion.

Later, I had the misconception that a positive attitude would eliminate all problems in life. I soon realized that was nonsense as well. Life will always give you plenty of problems, no matter how positive you might be.

Finally, I learned that a positive attitude is all about energy or fuel, and that energy or fuel helps me see things in a better light and do things in a better fashion. I learned that even though I may not *have* the best of everything, with a positive attitude, I can *make* the best of everything I have. And so can you. That's why a positive attitude always works.

What really pulled it together for me were the words of William Arthur Ward (1921–1994). In his book, *Fountains of Faith* (Anderson, SC: Droke House, 1970), Ward gives the most useful, realistic, and empowering definition of a positive attitude I've ever come across. He wrote, "Real optimism [or a positive attitude] is aware of problems but recognizes solutions, knows about difficulties but believes they can be overcome, sees the negatives but accentuates the positives, is exposed to the worst but expects the best, has reason to complain but chooses to smile."[11]

If you've got a positive attitude, you may still get down once in a while, but you won't stay there as long. You may still have some problems, but you'll get through them much more quickly. Your positive attitude propels you upward and pushes you forward. It's passion in its purest form.

As you integrate *The Champion Edge* into your life and work, you've learned about the power and practice of *purpose*. It's all about where you're going. But you also need passion to get you there, starting with the *attitude of passion*.

To keep on keeping on, you'll also need the *persistence of passion*. Read on.

CHAPTER 8

The Persistence of Passion

Persistence: The Oxygen Supply for Your Fire

I've compared passion to fire, and like any fire, it needs three components to work for you. The first component is fuel. That's your attitude. We talked about that in the last chapter. But to keep your passion fire burning, it also needs oxygen. That's *persistence*. With those two components in place, you're well on your way to getting more of *The Champion Edge* into your career and life.

Great minds throughout the ages have confirmed that. About two hundred years ago, the great American philosopher Ralph Waldo Emerson (1803–1882) said, "Every great success is ultimately the triumph of *persistence*."[1]

CEO and best-selling author Harvey Mackay says, "I've known entrepreneurs who were not great salespeople, or didn't know how to code, or were not particularly charismatic leaders. But I don't know of any entrepreneurs who have achieved any level of success without *persistence*."[2]

In 1985, the *Los Angeles Times* surveyed 120 top performers in business, sports, politics, entertainment, and academia. The one characteristic all these champions had in common is that they *persistently* worked to reach the top.[3]

Two of my former students, Scott Anderson and Chip Kudrle, who went on to form the Diamond Performance Group, have gotten very specific with this attribute as it applies to sales. They've found that 92 percent of salespeople give up after the fourth "no." Think about that. Ninety-two percent quit after the fourth "no"; however, 60 percent of customers say "no" four times *before* they say "yes." That means the majority of the sales go to the few salespeople who are *persistent* enough to hang in there and stay in contact with the prospect.

And my own experience in working with hundreds of thousands of people confirms that. The truly successful person or professional keeps on trying, *persistently*, despite the rejections, difficulties, and obstacles.

One of those customers, Jean, the president of a large construction company, told me, "In today's world, a successful leader or individual contributor must have *persistence*: persistence to weather the multitude of challenges that confront companies and individuals today."

If all the authorities seem to agree on the significance of *persistence*, then it must be extremely important and worthy of discussion. So what is it?

The Truth and Lies about Persistence

Persistence is keeping on—even when you don't feel like it. Pretty simple.

So what if you fall down? So what if you make a mistake? So what if you lose a customer, a business, a home, a relationship, or anything else that is vitally important to you? It's terrible, of course, but it's not the end of the world—if you practice persistence. You keep on keeping on no matter how you feel. You are determined to take the right actions, move in a positive direction, and pursue your goals, even though it may be easier to quit. That's what persistence is. That's the *truth*.

However, there are several *lies* that can trip you up, if you're not careful.

The first lie is that all you have to do is think your way to success. You can have whatever you want without doing anything. Some so-called experts even say that success is as simple as thinking about what you want and the results will magically appear. You know, "the secret" and "the law of attraction" and all that stuff. I disagree.

My research and experience tell me that it's critically important to *think* about the outcomes you want in a certain way in order to achieve them. We'll talk more about that later in the book. But I also know that thinking is a *part* of the success process, not the *entire* process. Persistent action must be there as well.

The second lie is that your success should come quickly and easily. After watching years of TV commercials, sitcoms, and dramas, many people have been conditioned to think that most of their health and beauty problems can be solved in 60 seconds. Other people have been conditioned to subconsciously think their career aspirations can be achieved in 60 minutes—or at least very quickly. And thus, all the hoopla about those "overnight successes." And all the disillusionment and discouragement when some newbies on the job can't figure out why they aren't further along in their careers. After all, in their mistaken minds, no persistence is necessary. But it's a lie.

And that lie can easily lead to quitting.

I'll never forget the time I was tempted to quit. It was my first paid speaking engagement at a major Fortune 500 company. I was hired to conduct a two-day seminar. Two hours into the program, the boss of the group called for a break, pulled me aside, and said, in effect, that I was a terrible speaker, offering none of the content he wanted. He proceeded to take over and teach the seminar for the next two days, as he relegated me to a seat in the back row. Talk about humiliation and failure.

I could have shut down my new, budding career as a professional speaker. I could have closed shop and gone back to my safer tenured career as a university professor. But I was lucky. I had a father who had taught me that even though I might fail at certain things in life, I was not a failure. I knew it was okay to fail, but it wasn't okay to give up.

My persistence paid off. Sometime later, another leader in that same company invited me for an interview. He wanted to discuss the possibility of hiring me to conduct a number of seminars for managers throughout their company. Before he continued the discussion further, I told him, in the spirit of total openness and honesty, that I had already spoken to another group in his company and had been promptly fired on the spot. He responded by thanking me for my disclosure, said he already knew about that incident, said the other guy was a "real jerk," and proceeded to give me a six-figure contract.

If I had folded up my company after that previous setback and humiliation, would I have gotten this big contract? Certainly not.

The *truth* is the achievements you and I see in champions are almost always preceded by a lot of blood, sweat, and tears. We *see* what looks like an overnight success, but we don't *hear* about the years of persistent guts and gumption that preceded it. When you read their stories, you can't help but conclude one thing: *Persistence is a major contributing factor in the results that are achieved.*

In fact, most of the time, persistence ensures your success. Some authors like H. Jackson Brown Jr. in *Life's Little Instruction Book* (Rutledge Hill Press, 1991) take it even further. He says, "In the confrontation between the stream and the rock, the stream *always* wins—not through strength but by perseverance." It's the combination of baby steps and persistence that brings about most victories in life.

The great singer Ray Charles (1930–2004) knew that. In fact, his whole life was a testament to the power of persistence. When he was six years old, he lost his eyesight. And to a young, poor blind child, the future didn't seem very promising.

But his mother told him, "Ray, you've lost your sight, but you haven't lost your mind. You can still create a productive life for yourself."

Ray began dreaming about becoming a music star. So he would practice the piano and practice his singing every day. One schoolteacher told him, "Ray, you can't play the piano, and God knows you can't sing. You'd better learn to weave chairs so you can support yourself."

That kind of feedback would have stopped most people dead in their tracks—but not Ray. He continued to focus on his goal of being a music star, even though time after time, in audition after audition, he was told he couldn't carry a tune in a bucket.

But here's the rest of the story. Ray Charles insisted on persisting. Eventually, he won 12 Grammys and was inducted into the Rock and Roll Hall of Fame for his musical talents. He performed for millions of ordinary people and hundreds of dignitaries around the world.

Certainly, Ray Charles was a gifted singer. But the world is filled with gifted singers who never go anywhere or become anybody, or as some would like to say, never make the big time.

So let me ask you: Was it Ray Charles' talent that brought him the Grammys? Yes, of course. But would he have gotten those Grammys if he hadn't persisted? Of course not.

Even Albert Einstein (1879–1955) who is always praised for his brilliance said, "It's not that I'm so smart; it's just that I stay with problems longer."[4]

The *truth* is most victories, on and off the job, are the result of persistence, not genius. And you can learn the art of persistence so you have *The Champion Edge* working for you. Check out the next five practices.

Persistence Practice #1: Tap into the Power of Desire

When you really, Really want something—a particular goal at work, a certain position in your career, or a certain achievement at home—your red-hot desire turns into persistence. Desire comes when you know your mighty "gotta-haves," not your milquetoast "nice-to-haves."

Buddha knew that. When a young man came to seek his advice, to discover the path of deliverance, Buddha led him down to the river. The young man assumed he was to undergo some ritual of purification. So they walked out into the river, and suddenly Buddha grabbed the man and held his head under the water.

The man struggled and fought. After a great deal of effort, the young man wrenched himself loose and brought his head above the water.

Quietly Buddha asked him, "When you thought you were drowning, what did you most desire?"

The young man gasped, "Air."

Buddha said, "When you want salvation as much as you want air, then you will get it."[5]

Likewise, when you really, Really want something, when you intensely *desire* some achievement in your business career or life, you will have the persistence you need to get the success you crave. So I've got five assignments for you. First, figure out your gotta-haves or your deepest desires. Second, write them down. Three, review your list every day. Add or subtract as necessary. Four, take a few seconds to think and dream about your desires every day. See them. Feel them. Taste them. Smell them. Five, repeat the process until your desire and persistence are sufficiently fired up.

Persistence Practice #2: Develop Resiliency

Persistence isn't something that somebody else can give you. Persistence isn't something you're born with. Plain and simple, it comes from a set of practices such as the ones we are discussing. And another one of those practices is a decision you make.

Decide to Get Back Up

When you're down, you decide to get back up. You may be at the bottom; you may land at the bottom, or you may have had others push you there. But you must also know that if you stay at the bottom, that's pretty much your decision, and it's certainly your responsibility. But a passionate persistent champion decides to get back up.

You see it over and over again. The first prizes don't always go to the most talented. They often go to the most determined. As the prolific journalist and civil rights activist Roscoe Dunjee (1883–1965) put it, "Some people succeed because they are destined to, but most people succeed because they are determined to."[6] They get back up.

Your getting-back-up ability plays a bigger role in your success than almost anything else. Business consultant John Baker has seen that so many times that he now says, "Durability is stronger than talent, better than luck, more real than potential, and more valuable than intellect." A great drive, or the decision to get back up, will easily compensate for little or limited talent.

And your resilience will be especially tested when you're faced with unfairness. After all, we all know deep down in our gut and high up in our head that life *should* be fair, but it isn't. But when it's not fair, it's easy to get sad, angry, demotivated, and depressed—all of which can kill your persistence.

So take a look at how you respond to unfair treatment. Someone else got the job or promotion that you deserved. Someone else got the credit for the work you did. And someone else got to take the trip you earned. Do you get down and out or up and going?

Refuse to Be a Victim

Champions, when they're the victim of unfair treatment, decide to keep on going anyway. One young lady learned that. While she was at Ohio State University, she set the goal of becoming Miss Ohio, not only for the title but also for the scholarship that would finance her college education. So she entered three pageants, three years in a row, and lost every one of them. But two days after the last event, the state pageant office called and said, "Laurel, the judges did not understand the ballot. We recounted and you won. But we've already crowned the other girl as the winner, and there is nothing we can do about it." How unfair.

Laurel could have sued. She could have spent months of negative energy plotting how to respond to the situation. But that's not what

Laurel did, because she understood at an amazingly young age, that life is not always fair. The best person doesn't always win. Mistakes can happen.

Rather than fret and stew, Laurel did something quite remarkable. She decided to try one more time. During her senior year in college, she entered the local pageant and won. She won Miss Ohio (1971), went to Atlantic City, and became Miss America (1972).[7]

The lesson is clear. You're more likely to get the results you want when you accept the fact that life is not always fair and keep on keeping on anyway.

Use Positive Phraseology

One of the best ways to reinforce your resiliency is to use "I can" language. What goes on in your head and what comes out of your mouth has a huge influence on your overall persistence. If, for example, you go around thinking, "It's too hard" or "It will never work," or if you find yourself saying, "I just can't do it" or "I can't hang in there any longer," you're in trouble. You've just shot down any measure of persistence you might have going for you.

However, when you talk to yourself positively, affirming the persistence you want and need to have (whether or not you already have it), you're going to become more persistent. There's incredible power in the use of affirmations. It's that simple and that magical. I cover more on that in a later chapter.

For the time being, to pump up your persistence, practice a lot of positive phraseology. Do what I have my students do. Tell yourself 20 times a day, "I can do it. I can do it. I can do it." Or "I keep on keeping on. I keep at it until I am finished and successful." Your words do matter.

Persistence Practice #3: Embrace Hard Work

Hard work is seldom popular. Most of us would like easy wins and instant successes. And if the payoff seems too far off in the future, many people just throw in the towel.

Champions embrace hard work by recognizing that *the size of the payoff is what really counts,* not the length of time it will take to accomplish.

Champions embrace hard work because they also know success is not measured by being the very best at something. That would leave most of us out. They embrace hard work because they know *success is measured by doing your best with what you have.*

Do Your Best with What You Have

Take Joe Frazier (1944–2011), for example. As a young boy, Joe dreamed of becoming a boxer. He got an old sack and filled it with sand. That was his punching bag. And that was the beginning of his disciplined plan to reach the success he wanted. Eventually, he won the gold medal for boxing at the Olympic Games.

When asked about his secret, he said that success depends on your roadwork. You must be willing to do your roadwork, week after week, month after month, and hurdle after hurdle. You can get anywhere you want to go if you are willing to work hard.

What many people don't know is that Joe had a handicap. His left arm was injured when he was a small boy. The injury left him unable to completely extend his left arm.

As John Shumway, a former amateur boxer told me, "I can tell you with confidence that one of the most important assets a boxer has is his left-hand jab. The jab is not only an indispensable defensive weapon, but it is the cornerstone of a boxer's offense. At the incredibly competitive and dangerous world-class level of professional boxing, a left-hand jab is crucial."

If you watch the way Joe Frazier fought, you see that Joe did not effectively utilize his left jab. The limited range of motion of his left arm was not suited to the jab. Instead, he did the best he could with what he had.

So as a boy, punching a bag of sand, he threw thousands of left hooks—a punch for which his left arm was suited. He also believed that if he could develop superior endurance, he could win in the ring.

Because of Joe's persistence, his tireless hard work, and his willingness to adapt, he became a great champion. Joe combined his lethal left hook with a fearless and unrelenting style to get to the top of the boxing world.

When Joe Frazier fought Muhammad Ali, he was up against the best left jab anyone had ever seen. Nonetheless, for 15 rounds, Frazier stalked Ali, firing his deadly left hook while tirelessly bobbing under Ali's lightning-fast punches. Frazier wore down Ali, actually dropping him to the canvas with his wicked left hook late in the fight. Although Ali was able to fight to the end, he was unable to sustain an effective offense. Joe Frazier became the heavyweight champion of the world and one of the most respected fighters to ever step into the ring.[8]

Frazier did the best he could with what he had. This is one of the keys to persistence. Are you doing the best with what you have? If so, you've got some more of *The Champion Edge* working for you.

Unfortunately, many people aren't doing the best they can with what they have. They compare their talent to someone else's, and when they find themselves lacking, they give up. This is the student who thinks, "I'll never be as smart as Theodore, so why even bother to try?" Or it's the salesperson who thinks, "I'll never be in the top 10 percent of this company's sales force, so why should I be working so hard? I'll just get by, and that's good enough."

No, it isn't. If you don't make the best of what you do have, you'll have even less—less self-esteem, less self-respect, less happiness, less success, and less of everything else that might be valuable.

Practice and Then Practice Some More

Champions embrace hard work because they know practice precedes payoff. Even before he became a professional basketball star, Bob Pettit understood the power of practice. He knew that the achievements he wanted would come as the result of practice, practice, and more practice. Even though he became one of the highest scoring players in the sport, it wasn't that way in the beginning.

As a freshman in high school, Bob was weak, frail, and uncoordinated. All he had going for him was the determination to practice until he became a quality athlete.

Bob began with a wire coat hanger that he bent into the shape of a basketball hoop. Hour after hour, day after day, he threw tennis balls through his makeshift basket. Eventually, his father got him a real basketball and hoop.

Bob would throw baskets after school every day, go to dinner, and then go back to practice. It wasn't too long before he became the star of his church team, then his high school team, college team, and finally a professional team. He became the first recipient of the NBA's Most Valuable Player (MVP) award. And he won the NBA All-Star Game MVP award four times,[9] a feat matched only by Kobe Bryant.

It's the same for you and me. You've got to embrace hard work, which means you've got to practice your craft over and over again. So ask yourself, "Are you practicing enough?" If your answer is "yes," congratulations! You know something about the power of persistence.

But you may be saying, "I don't even know how to practice. And even if I did, there are times I don't feel like practicing." Then try this. The next time you're working on a task you know you have to do but don't want to, give it your all for 10 minutes. No matter how distasteful the task, I know you can give it your best for 10 minutes. The next time you're back on that or any other disliked task, give it your all for 15 minutes. Keep on adding five minutes to these practice sessions, and you will often find that you want to go on longer. Then you'll know that you are in the process of mastering persistence.

From all these stories, you probably realize one thing. Persistence pays off in the long run. Your success may not come immediately, but your success is fairly certain if you persist. That's why it's very important to also practice patience.

Persistence Practice #4: Apply Patience

It's a toughie. Most of us are like the person who prayed to God, "I want patience, now!" It's difficult to stay calm and patient, but it's a vital part of persistence.

If you want to be a champion, if you want phenomenal success, it will be hard. What else could you possibly expect? If it wasn't hard, everyone would be doing it.

Refuse to Be Sidetracked

If you're not the patient type, you can learn to be patient and apply patience—by refusing to be sidetracked. Pain, setbacks, tragedies, disappointments, sickness, and other adversities are always chasing you.

At least three or four times a year, one or more of those things will catch up to you or someone you care about. And if you're not careful, they'll distract or sidetrack you, taking your persistence with them.

You can't allow that to happen. You can stay patient and on course if you refuse to be sidetracked. Senator Robert Taft (1889–1953) demonstrated that. Early in his political career, he went into hostile territory to make a speech. Someone threw an overripe tomato at him. It hit the senator in the chest and burst all over his face, glasses, and hair.

What did he do? React with anger? Lash out? Quit? No. He didn't wipe his face, glasses, or hair. He just went on giving his speech and never even referred to the tomato. When he finished, he stepped down from the platform and said, "Good-bye boys," in a friendly manner. As Senator Taft walked down the aisle toward the door, the once hostile crowd gave him a standing ovation.

That's what I call class on the senator's part. And that's how persistent people get through adversity and onto the payoffs. They refuse to get sidetracked.

Could the same be said of you? Do you stay calm and remain patient? Do you refuse to give up? Do you endure?

Or do people, secretly behind your back, say you bail out when things get a little tough? Do they say you give up way too easily or throw in the towel too quickly? Do they point out the fact that you seldom finish what you start?

If you answer "yes" to any of these questions about how others view you, let me tell you once again—you can learn patience.

Do a Cost and Benefit Analysis

Try this exercise. Write the name of your challenge or desired goal at the top of a sheet of paper. Put a line down the middle.

At the top of the left-hand column, write down the words, "What it will cost me if I quit." Write down all the losses you will incur if you quit. Maybe you will lose some time, money, energy, promotions, and relationships. At the top of the right-hand column, write down the words "What are the benefits I will receive if I persist?"

You'll discover, most of the time, that you have a lot more to gain and very little to lose by not quitting and applying patience to your situation. As Benjamin Franklin put it, "He that can have patience can have what he will."[10]

Persistence Practice #5: Reject Defeat

Failure and defeat aren't easy. I know. I've failed in relationships. I've failed in business. And I've failed in a dozen other ways, as well, on various occasions. And maybe you have too.

Well, so what! Far worse than failure and defeat is failing to persist because you *might* fail. Yes, that's possible, but that's also a stupid way to approach life.

To keep on keeping on, you must learn to reject defeat. Sounds nice in theory, but how do you do that?

Give Your Feelings a Vote but Not a Veto

Of course, there will be times when you will not *feel* like doing what you need to do. There will be times when you don't feel like hanging in there. But be a little wary of your feelings. They can sometimes be useful in decision making, but they should never have the final say in whether you continue doing what needs to be done. The final say should come from a thoughtful consideration of your purpose and the payoffs you want to achieve as well as a look at what your head and heart are telling you about whether to keep on or quit.

That's what Lucille did. Even though she didn't *feel* like going on, *she rejected defeat by not allowing her feelings to veto her dreams.*

It all started when she told her friends she was going to be an actress. So she went off to drama school in New York City at the age of 16. But it wasn't too long before her mother received a letter from the school saying, "Take her home. She has no acting ability whatsoever."

Her feelings said, "Quit. Forget about it." But how could she go home? She had told all her friends she was going to be an actress.

So she auditioned as a showgirl in a musical and got the job without pay. Four weeks before opening night she was fired. She then auditioned for three other musicals, and each time she was hired and fired before opening night. Talk about obstacles. In two years she had not earned one penny as an actress.

Finally, she got a job as a model, but that didn't last long. She came down with pneumonia, which resulted in severe, long-term pain in both legs. The doctor said she might never walk again and sent her to a New York City hospital as a charity case, where she spent the next several months. While there, she hobbled around on crutches, then used a cane, having to wear 20-pound weights on her shoes. It was two years before she was well again.

Talk about defeats. She had gone to New York City at 16, and now, by age 22, she had nothing to show for herself except a track record of persistence and the lessons she learned from rejecting defeats.

And yet some years later, in 1953, according to a June 2, 2013, entry on the National Media Museum blog, 20 million people watched the coronation of Queen Elizabeth on TV. Twenty-nine million people watched TV as Dwight Eisenhower was inaugurated as president. And yet 44 million people watched this star of the TV show *I Love Lucy* in the much-anticipated episode from season 2, "Lucy Goes to the Hospital."[11]

The actress, of course, was Lucille Ball. From the very first episode, when she was 40, her show was rated as one of the top 10 TV shows in America. And within 20 episodes, it became the number-one show in America, where it remained for four years.[12]

So was Lucille Ball a success or a failure? If you read her fascinating life story, you realize she was both. But ultimately, she was a success because *she rejected defeat by giving her feelings a voice in her career but not the final word.*

Renounce Negative Self-Talk

Taking it a step further, to actively and vigorously reject defeat, renounce negative self-talk. You and I will have some failures along the way. That's a given. But don't ever tell yourself, "I'm a failure." You are not defined by an incident or two or three, or even an ongoing bad habit. As psychologist Dr. Bev Smallwood tells her clients, "You are definitely not a 'failure,' *unless* you bail out, give up, or quit trying." And I might add, "Unless you *call* yourself a failure."

Champions renounce negative self-talk. Bruce Lee (1940–1973), the martial artist, actor, and author, is a prime example of this. He said, "Defeat is a state of mind. No one is ever defeated until defeat has been accepted as reality."[13]

When I'm tempted to give up and throw in the towel, when I begin to think negatively—that I'm never going to make it—I give myself a firm reprimand. I renounce the negative self-talk by telling myself, "Stop it! Now just stop it!" And I replace the negative self-talk with a positive affirmation. I tell myself, over and over again, "Never let up when you're ahead; never give up when you're behind."

Ask yourself, "How are you going to renounce any negative self-talk that threatens to kill off your *Champion Edge* persistence?"

Your Challenge

As we finish this chapter, I'm reminded of the coach who was talking to his football team. He was talking about the kind of players he wanted to recruit. He asked them, "Men, do we want the kind of player who gets knocked down and stays down?" They all shouted, "No!"

The coach asked, "Do we want the player who gets knocked down, gets up once, gets knocked down again, and stays down?" Again the men shouted, "No!"

So the coach continued, "Do we want the player who keeps getting knocked down and keeps getting up?" The players said, "Yes!"

Of course, that's not too bad. But the coach said, "No. I want the player who keeps knocking him down."

You need to be both of those players—the one who keeps on getting up and keeps on knocking down the obstacles that get in your way. And you will be one of those champions when you've got the power of persistence working for you.

CHAPTER 9

The Character of Passion

Character: The Guidance System for Your Fire

If I asked you to name one of the biggest con artists of the past 100 years, or if I asked you who operated one of the biggest Ponzi schemes of all time, you'd probably name Bernie Madoff. He scammed thousands of people out of billions of dollars and was eventually sent to prison. While he was there, he was asked how he felt about his past as a con artist and his present as a jailbird. His response was alarming as well as refreshing. He said, "I've never been at more peace in my life. My lack of character was killing me."

Madoff *looked* and *sounded* like a man of passion, which is the second element in *The Champion Edge*. He had plenty of attitude—the fuel to feed his fire. He had an abundance of persistence—the oxygen that kept his fire burning. But he lacked the third component of passion—the *character* or the guidance system for his fire. As a result, his fire burned out of control and devastated the futures of countless people and organizations, as well as his own.

As I've said in the last three chapters, passion is very similar to fire. It needs fuel or attitude to get you going. It needs oxygen or persistence to keep you moving. But it also needs a guidance system, like a fire ring or a fireplace, to keep you moving in the right direction. That's the role of character.

And all champions have it. In fact, by its very definition, if you have every portion of *The Champion Edge* working for you except character, you would be a loser.

What Is Character?

Many famous people have talked about the importance of character. Kitty Carlisle Hart (1910–2007), the film and TV star, said, "A career takes more than talent. It takes character." And evangelist Billy Graham preached, "When wealth is lost, nothing is lost; when health is lost, something is lost; when character is lost, all is lost."

I believe your character will prove to be more important than your career. After all, your character is one of the few things you take with you wherever you go in life. And some would argue it's the only thing you take with you when you leave this life.

In the 1700s, abolitionist John Woolman *equated it with walking your talk*. He said, "Conduct is more convincing than language."[1] A person of character walks his talk. What he says and what he does are in sync with one another.

During the Great Depression, humorist Will Rogers (1879–1935) *equated it with upright, moral behavior*. He told people to "live in such a way that you wouldn't be ashamed to sell your parrot to the town gossip!"[2]

In the late 20th century, theologian Dr. Charles Swindoll *equated character with courage*, but not the heroic acts of courage witnessed on the battlefield. He equated character with the quieter forms of courage, such things as "remaining faithful when nobody's looking, like enduring pain when the room is empty, like standing alone when you're misunderstood."[3]

Character has several ingredients. But when it comes to *The Champion Edge*, I define Level 1 character as *doing the right thing*.

Better yet is Level 2 character: *doing the right thing, when nobody's watching*. One of my business clients, Hearth and Home Technologies calls it "personal integrity," and they demand that all their salespeople do is right even "when no one is watching."

British historian Thomas B. Macaulay (1800–1859) wrote very much the same thing about 150 years ago, "The measure of a man's real character is what he would do if he knew he would never be found out."[4] And Congressman J. C. Watts Jr. declared, "Character is doing what's right when nobody's looking."[5]

Level 3 character goes even a step further: *doing the right thing, even when it costs something*. William Clay Ford Jr., chief executive at the Ford Motor Company, demonstrated that awhile back. When Ford Motor stock was downgraded, Ford told the company shareholders that he would not accept any compensation until profits from the automotive division improved.

Wow! Usually we read just the opposite. When a company's fortunes fall, the leadership team members still earn huge amounts of money at the same time the employees lose jobs, benefits, and pensions—the very opposite of character. Not Ford. He was *doing the right thing,* even when it cost something.

Of course, that begs the question.

How Do You Know If You're Doing the Right Thing?

It's not real complicated. You don't even need an MBA or a PhD in business ethics to figure out if you're doing the right thing.

This may sound oversimplified, but I'll give you an answer that is correct 99 percent of the time. *You're doing the right thing if you're comfortable having other people know about your behavior—along with all your thoughts behind that behavior.* Or put another way, if your behavior and motivations were broadcast on TV or printed on the front page of the newspaper, you would be okay with that.

If you would prefer to have your intentions and actions kept private, however, chances are you've got a character problem. The more you want to hide your behavior, the less right it's likely to be. The more willing you are to have your thoughts, decisions, rationales, and behaviors exposed, the more right they're likely to be.

That's one way to know if you're *doing the right thing.* Give yourself a gut check. The other way is to get the feedback of others.

Get Feedback on Your Character

As Joseph M. Tucci, the CEO of the information management firm EMC, says, "Every move you make, everything you say, is visible to all."[6] And management consultant Darcy Hitchcock says, "Employees are professional boss watchers."[7] They don't miss a thing you say or do.

That means your bosses, coworkers, subordinates, customers, and even your spouse and kids know a great deal about your character. They've been watching you. And they have probably been talking about you behind your back. They know exactly what they think about your character. The question is, have you even bothered to ask them?

You need to get some feedback. Find out how you're coming across to the people you lead, live with, and work with. It takes courage to ask for feedback, and it takes guts to listen to their answers without getting defensive. But you need to ask them nonetheless.

Ask some of your colleagues, coworkers, customers, friends, and relatives such questions as:

- What words would you use to describe me to someone else? Where would the words "character, integrity, honorable, and upright" fall on that list?
- On a scale of 1 to 10, where ten is the best, how would you score my trustworthiness—to tell the truth and do what I say I'm going to do?
- What does my example "tell" other people?
- Where do I seem to be lacking in character? Or where does there seem to be a gap between what I say and what I do?
- What is there in my character that automatically earns your trust? And what is there in my character that automatically alerts your danger signals?
- If I were to have a character makeover, what changes do I need to make?
- What three things in my character do you find to be the most admirable?

Take the time to get some feedback, to see if you're *doing the right thing*, to see if people see you as a champion with character. If you like what you discover, great. If you find that your character needs some development, you can develop your character. Let's get started. There are essentially two approaches to character building, both of which are needed to fire up your career success and life.

Character Building 101: Show Respect for the Truth

The first thing other people want to see in you is *you,* not some superficial image you've created and tried to project, in person or on social media.

Be Authentic

That's why the first way you show respect for the truth is by being authentic. Of course, this practice might seem so elementary that I shouldn't even have to mention it. But we're living in a time when looking good (and putting the right spin on things) seems to be more important than being good and being real.

As a professor teaching a class on "Communication between the Sexes," I was forever cautioning my students about the way some of them approached their dating relationships. Rather than being themselves, some of them would try to figure out what kind of person would be most attractive to someone of the opposite sex, and then they would pretend to be that kind of person.

That approach always fails on two counts. First of all, you won't like yourself for doing it. In fact, you can't possibly like yourself if you don't even accept yourself.

Second, the other person won't like you either. You can't be the Great Pretender forever. Eventually, your real self will be revealed, and from then on, the other person will automatically question everything you say and do because you're not engaging in behaviors that show a respect for the truth.

To be authentic, you have to be absolutely clear about who you are and what you stand for—in business, in your career, and in your life. You have to know your values, and you have to live your values.

Be Honest

If you're going to have *The Champion Edge* working for you, you can't play games with the truth. You must be absolutely honest. No distortions. No little white lies. No false fronts. No bravado. No parsing of words, such as the definition of "is." Character comes out in plain, simple, but tactful, honesty.

The strange thing is most people think they are honest, but they don't think there's anything wrong with a little dishonesty. They rationalize that white lies, exaggerations, or minor distortions of the truth are okay.

But what would you think of a manager who says, "My staff is really upset about the company's new quality initiative," but later you discover there had been only one, minor complaint? Obviously, you wouldn't trust that manager quite as much in the future. As the German philosopher Friedrich Nietzsche (1844–1900) said, "What upsets me is not that you lied to me, but that from now on I can no longer believe you."[8]

The cold stark reality is—*anything other than absolute honesty does not exhibit character and does not build trust.*

That's how I live my life and run my business now and how I have for the past several decades. But there was a brief time in my life when I failed that test. I was working my way through my undergraduate degree as a shoe salesman in a women's department store. I sold out my character on those nights I stayed late so we could mark *up* all the prices on our shoes before the big sale the following day. My coworkers and I put a "New Sale Price" label on each box of shoes that was the same as the old, original, full-price offer. I sold out my character when I lied to my customers about how much money they were saving when they bought the shoes. I couldn't look my customers in the eye; I couldn't speak to them with confidence, and I couldn't live with myself behaving that way. So I quickly decided I would treat the truth with the respect it deserved.

To make things worse, business paralysis sets in when people are afraid to tell the truth. As Margaret Heffernan, former CEO at CMGI, states, "I've seen countless deals hang in midair because no one had the honesty to say out loud what everyone was thinking privately: 'This is really stupid' and 'It will never work.' And so millions of dollars and countless hours of work were lost somewhere between intent and execution, with people in the know hoping that the whole mess will simply go away, but remaining unwilling to address the problem head on."[9]

Some people have a problem with honesty. Do you? Do you find it easier to tell the embellished truth? Do you ever give a presentation that only includes the "facts" that support your predetermined version of the truth while leaving out the other "facts?" Do you craft your words to "give the right impression"—even though that impression may not be accurate? If so, you're not giving truth the respect it deserves. If you are going to show respect for the truth, you have to be honest. That doesn't mean you're cruel, brutal, and tactless because that would violate the other character-building practice of showing respect for others.

You have to be honest, nonetheless. It is at the foundation of every good, healthy, and effective relationship. Other people don't know when a lie is so small that it's okay and when a lie is so big that it's not okay. They simply want you to be a person who respects the truth by telling the truth.

Keep Your Word

Champions always do this: they make commitments, and they do what they say they're going to do.

And, "Yes, keeping your word is sometimes difficult, expensive, and inconvenient," according to Michael Hyatt, the former chairman and CEO of Thomas Nelson Publishers, and author of *Platform: Get Noticed in a Noisy World* (Thomas Nelson, 2012). "But the cost of not doing so is even *more expensive.* It will ultimately cost you your leadership."[10]

Non-champions use noncommittal language instead. They'll say, "I'll see . . ." "I'll think about it . . ." and "Well, maybe . . ." And if they ever do make any commitments, what they really mean is, "Sure, I'll do it, if nothing else comes up, if I don't get a better offer, and if I feel like it." Which is a far cry from making a commitment and then keeping your word.

If you're going to be a champion filled with passion and guided by character, if you're going to lead a team or an organization, if you're going to lead a family, you've got to keep your word. No excuses. You know that a promise is a promise. It doesn't matter if you no longer "feel" like doing what you said you were going to do. Unless all hell breaks out, if you're a person of character, you keep your word. You follow through on every promise you make.

As one person noted, "Character is the ability to follow through on a resolution . . . long after the mood in which it was made . . . has left you." Champions don't let their feelings rule their lives; they rule their feelings by thoughtful, conscientious decision making and follow-through.

Admit Your Mistakes

Even if you do what you think is right, you're going to be wrong some of the time. And champions of character admit their mistakes. They don't pass the buck. And they don't blame anybody else or anything else *if* they are indeed responsible. When you admit your mistakes, you show respect for the truth.

I remember one high school principal who made a serious mistake, and everyone in the school knew he made a serious mistake. He got on the intercom and apologized to the entire student body even though he was concerned about losing everyone's respect as a result of his mistake and his apology. He became the most popular and respected high school principal in the district. Months afterward, students came up to him and said they wished they had a father like him, as their fathers couldn't ever admit they were wrong.

Katie Paine, founder and CEO of the Delahaye Group, instinctively knew that. She instituted the "Mistake of the Month Club." She says, "Several years ago, I overslept and missed a flight to a big client meeting. I walked into my next staff meeting, plunked $50 down on the table, and said, 'If you can top this mistake, that money is yours.'"

Katie continued, "People started to own up to mistakes, and suddenly we had a flood of them. At every staff meeting since, we've set aside 3 minutes to write up the mistakes of the month on a whiteboard. Then we cast a vote. Since then we've recorded more than two thousand mistakes. Once a mistake hits the whiteboard, it tends not to happen again. It has become a bonding ritual. Once you go through it, you're a member of the club."[11]

Admitting your mistakes takes guts. But it also displays character and demonstrates your respect for the truth.

Character Building 201: Show Respect for Others

The comedian Rodney Dangerfield made his living by talking about the fact he never got any respect from anyone. We can laugh, but in reality, it's not funny if you feel disrespected by others. However, when you're a champion of character—doing what's right—you make deliberate behavior choices that demonstrate your respect for others.

Give Rather Than Take

First, you show respect for others when you give to them rather than take from them. The great actress Katharine Hepburn (1907–2003) talked about that. She said, "Love has nothing to do with what you are expecting to get—only what you are expecting to give."[12] The same truth applies to character and respect.

Givers think about others, and their thoughtfulness shows up in their respectful behavior. One of my customers, Deb Wittenberg, the manager of Learning and Development for the Digi-Key Corporation, was like that. When I asked her for her definition of a giver, she said, "It's all about 'paying it forward.' I feel successful when the way I behaved, the way I spoke, and the way I listened to someone's concerns affected another person's life in such a way that he or she made better, more positive decisions."

Alternatively, you're a disrespectful taker if you're a leader who seldom thinks about how the corporate changes will affect your staff or seldom asks for their input. You're a taker if you're a customer service provider who treats customers as an interruption of your work instead of being the main reason for your work. And you're a taker if you're so preoccupied with your iPhone, iPad, Instagram, Twitter, and TV programs that you fail to connect with your family members.

Are you more of a giver or a taker? Champions are always more of a giver than a taker type.

Assume Good Intentions

Second, you show respect for others when you assume good intentions on their part. It's easy to get upset with people who irritate us. And it's easy to give them disrespect in return.

Take complaining customers, for example. At Charles Schwab, the investment company, they assume that a complaining customer is simply a person with a problem who wants help in fixing their problem. They assume the other person has good intentions. So they welcome complaints and try to see things from the other person's point of view, rather than immediately react to the other person's sometimes offensive behavior. Because they know that a well-handled complaint turns into extra sales for the company. More than half of their complaining customers give them even more business after their complaint.

By contrast, I think of one manager who assumed the worst. He noticed that one of his employees habitually left five minutes earlier than she was supposed to. At about 4:50 p.m., she started to clear her desk, and at 4:55 p.m. she bolted out the door.

This particular manager hated this behavior. It was unacceptable, and on several occasions, he had thought of firing her. What restrained him was the fact that on all other accounts she was an excellent employee.

One day, however, the manager's resentment built to the point where he simply had to confront her. He called her into his office and told her that her early departures had not gone unnoticed. He asked if she had any explanation.

She said, "Yes, I believe I have. I am a widow with three small children. The woman who cares for them during the day must leave at 5:45. If I catch the 5:00 bus, I get home at 5:45. If I don't get on that bus, the next bus doesn't leave until 5:45, and that gets me home at 6:30. I can't leave three small children unattended for 45 minutes. I didn't want to tell you because I was afraid I would have to leave my job."

The manager was no longer incensed or irritated. He moved from a jumped conclusion to a fuller understanding. He promptly made special arrangements for her to leave five minutes early each day and make up the time on special occasions.

Character is exhibited when you *start* your interactions with someone else, assuming good intentions on their part, because that kicks your respectful behavior into gear.

Practice Kindness

Third, you show respect for others when you are kind. As author Michael Josephson points out, "The way we treat people we think can't help or hurt us (like housekeepers, waiters, and secretaries), tells more about our character than how we treat people we think are important. People who are honest, kind, and fair only when there's something to gain shouldn't be confused with people of real character who demonstrate these qualities habitually, under all circumstances. Character is not a fancy coat we put on for show. It's who we really are."[13]

I know what he's talking about when he refers to how we treat those "less important" people. In the early days of my career, when I was finishing my doctoral studies and writing my dissertation, I worked as a part-time instructor at the university to make some money to support my wife and child. And not to boast, but I was a natural at teaching. I was really good at it. Students sat there in rapt attention and furiously took notes on all the brilliant things I had to say. I felt respected.

But money was very short. So I got another part-time job as a desk clerk at a hotel working from 11 p.m. to 7 a.m. I was stunned by the way some of the customers treated me. I experienced everything from condescending tones of voice and rolling eyes to verbal putdowns. This was anything but kindness. I couldn't believe the contrast in treatment. A few hours before I had been *the* respected rising star in academia being quoted by others, and now, I was one of *those* lowly servants.

What about you? Do you treat everyone with kindness, no matter what his or her title, position, or profit potential might be? Or do you sometimes treat people as things to be used in the pursuit of your goals? *The Champion Edge* has a distinctive kind note about it.

Serve Others

Fourth, you show respect for others when you serve them. Sounds something like "servant leadership," doesn't it? And it sounds very much like some fourth-grade children Robert Roberts writes about where the teacher introduced a game called "balloon stomp." A balloon was tied to every child's leg, and the object of the game was to pop everyone else's balloon while guarding your own. The last person with an unpopped balloon would win.

The first group wasted no time in entering into the spirit of the game. Balloons were relentlessly targeted and destroyed, and the entire battle was quickly over. It's hard to win at a game like balloon stomp because you're almost forced to be pushy, rude, and offensive.

But then a second class was introduced to the same game. Only this time it was a class of intellectually disabled children. They were given the same explanation as the first class, but the game was played very differently. Perhaps the instructions were given too quickly for children with learning disabilities to grasp them. The one idea that got through was that the balloons were supposed to be popped. So it was the balloons, rather than the other players, that were viewed as enemies. Instead of fighting each other, the children began helping each other pop balloons. One little girl knelt down and held her balloon carefully in place, like a holder for a field goal kicker. A little boy stomped it flat. Then he knelt down and held his balloon for her. It went on like this for several minutes until all the balloons were vanquished, and everybody cheered. Everybody won.[14]

Who got the game right, and who got the game wrong? In our world, we tend to think of another person's success as one less opportunity for us to succeed. There can only be one top dog, one top banana, one big kahuna. If we ever find ourselves in that enviable position, we will fight like mad to maintain our hold on it. A lot of people and a lot of companies fail to enjoy prolonged success because they have this balloon-stomp mentality, instead of a character-minded mentality of serving others.

How are you playing the game? It's worth a moment of your time to reflect on the question.

The Good and the Bad News about Character

The Bad News

As journalist Richard Reeves notes, "All leaders face some crisis where their own strength of character is the enemy." He should have said, "*Everybody* will face crises where their own strength of character is the enemy." Your character will be tested.

You're going to have those times when it would be quicker and easier to criticize a coworker in public rather than wait for a more appropriate and private moment. Your character will help you decide which way you go—with expediency or respect.

You're going to have those times when you're tempted to tell your salespeople to say whatever they have to say to make the sale, even though it means "stretching the truth." Your character will help you decide which way you go—with profit or honesty.

You're going to have those times when you want to say you're out of the office when you're there, or you didn't receive a message when you did. Your character will help you decide which way you go—with a cover-up or transparency.

You're going to have those pressure-filled times when *doing the right thing* may seem too laborious. Does your character push you toward doing the right thing all the time? Or does your character take a nosedive when you think no one is looking or it's going to cost you something?

The Good News

You get to choose the kind of character you want to bring to your career and business and life. As Heraclitus of Ephesus says, "The content of your character is your choice. Day by day, what you choose, what you think, and what you do is who you become. Your integrity is your destiny."

Character is doing what's right, all the time, whether or not it's cool, popular, expedient, or politically correct. As journalist Walter Lippmann (1889–1974) noted, champions hold themselves "to an ideal of conduct even when it is inconvenient, unprofitable, or dangerous to do so."[15] And as a champion, you go beyond looking out for yourself and do what is right for all concerned, as much as possible. It keeps your passion from turning into greed, selfishness, or fanaticism. That's good news.

So far, we've talked about the *power of purpose*—where *The Champion Edge* begins. And we've talked about the *power of passion*—where *The Champion Edge* gets fired up. But it's time we look at the *power of process*, where your actions turn into results.

PART III

Process

CHAPTER 10

The Power of Process

Where *The Champion Edge* Turns into Results

You remember *The Champion Edge* that helps you accomplish so much more so much faster is composed of three skill sets: purpose, passion, and process.

We've spent considerable time talking about purpose, which is all about direction, and passion, which is all about energy. So let's dig into the third and final element—*process*, which is all about the skills or methods that help you achieve your desired results.

How I Learned about Process

My introduction to *the power of process* came at age seven. I was visiting with Judy, my nine-year-old next-door neighbor and my secret crush. As we were sitting on the lawn talking, I noticed a medium-sized cardboard box sitting next to her, with a collection of smaller boxes strewn around it. Of course, I was curious and asked her what that was all about.

Judy explained that she had ordered a sample collection of greeting cards that she had seen advertised in a comic book. The ad said all she had to do was go knocking on doors, show the person who answered the door her selection of cards, take orders for those cards, and make *big* money. But she had changed her mind and no longer wanted to do that.

No problem. I wanted to do it! I wanted to make some of that big money, which was probably not more than $20 to $30 back then. So I asked Judy if I could sell her sample collection if she wasn't going to. She readily agreed.

Within 10 minutes, I was knocking on doors, talking to people, showing them my greeting cards, and taking orders. When I got home that night for dinner, I was mighty proud of myself. I told my parents about my new business and showed them the number of orders I had gotten. I never even thought about asking for their permission or guidance; I just did it.

Although my parents were impressed with my initiative, my father was particularly interested in how I was going to manage my business. He asked me a number of questions about how I had conducted myself with my prospects, how I would fulfill the orders I received, and what thought I had given to profit margins. Of course, I had not given any thought to any of those business issues. I just knocked on doors and said, "You wouldn't want to buy any cards, would you?"

My father questioned me to make sure this was what I really wanted to do—spend my summer vacation selling greeting cards. I let him know that I was serious. I was in business to be successful and make some money. I had a goal—to buy the awesome three-speed Schwinn bicycle I saw in the window of the Montgomery Ward department store. It was a child's dream bicycle, but I also knew it was a bike my truck-driver father and homemaker mother could never afford to buy me.

Once my father was convinced of my commitment, he let me know there was a better way to run my business than the way I had done it that very first day. He told me there were several *processes* I needed to learn and use if I was going to maximize my profits and produce the success I wanted.

Of course, I had never heard of the word *processes* let alone know how I could use them in my tiny startup business. And so my training began with my father. And it has continued every day of my life since then. Through the pursuit of my undergraduate and graduate degrees. Through the attainment of the CSP (Certified Speaking Professional), the highest earned award of the National Speakers Association. Through my attendance at hundreds of educational conferences, seminars, and workshops. And through my research that has resulted in the publication of several books and more than 1,000 articles.

But back to my father and his teaching of business processes. It started with my thoughts. He indicated that I had to be committed to selling the greeting cards and believe I could sell them, in huge quantities to lots of customers. In a sense, he was introducing me to *the process of affirming achievement*, which we'll address in Chapter 11. And somewhat accidentally I started telling myself positive affirmations, telling myself I could do it, that I was a success, and that I was a successful businessperson. My closing rate shot up instantly and dramatically. Almost everyone said "yes," that they would like to see my greeting cards, and almost everyone purchased.

My father also taught me that too many salespeople fail to sell because they haven't worked on their presentation. They don't know to communicate with their prospects to get the cooperation they want. (You'll hear more about this in Chapter 12: The Process of Connective Communication.) I couldn't simply go to a door and "wing it." I had to have a prepared presentation instead of just saying whatever came out of my mouth.

So we began to work on my presentation, word for word, sentence by sentence, writing it all down. Then it was my job to practice my little presentation over and over again until it was memorized, smooth, and conversational. I don't know if my sales improved because my presentation was refined or because my housewife prospects were impressed that a seven-year-old sounded so professional. I suspect it was a bit of both. That was the first summer with my new business.

By age nine, when my third summer vacation came around, I still wanted to be in the greeting card business. But it was time for some additional teaching. My father taught me if I wanted to get more from my customers, I would have to listen for their expressed or unexpressed needs. My customers had been telling me they would be interested in such things as wrapping paper, and my vendor had a very attractive, full-color catalog that featured everything from wrapping paper, to kitchen gadgets, wall plaques, knickknacks, and a host of gift items. But I hadn't been listening. I just kept on doing business the way I had been doing it the last couple of years.

Even though he didn't use these exact words, my father was talking about the *process of compassionate listening*, the subject for Chapter 13. I started to listen and my business prospered. Indeed, I was buying so many products from my vendor and selling so much merchandise that the president of the company called my house. She spoke to my mother, asking if she could speak to Alan Zimmerman, who had become their company's biggest customer. She wanted to know what my secret was; she wanted me to share it with their other customers so they could learn from me.

Of course, she had no idea she was about to speak to a 10-year-old kid. I couldn't articulate my secret then as I can now, but I had been using

The Champion Edge. I had a *purpose*, no matter how meager it may have been originally, getting a bicycle, then moving on to the larger purpose of saving for a car, and then pursuing the substantial purpose of saving for college. I had plenty of *passion* to keep me going, and my father was teaching me the *processes* I needed to know to bring it all together.

Something surprising and wonderful happened. I was on fire. *The Champion Edge* was working and propelling me on to higher and higher levels of achievement. I added an import division to my little door-to-door business. I began importing cuckoo clocks from Germany, watches from France, shoes from Eastern Europe, and a host of other goods. It was an early and valuable introduction to how *The Champion Edge* works.

Do you have that kind of fire in you? Do you have *TCE* working its magic in your career and life? If not, you may be lacking in *process*. Part III of this book may be the missing piece.

Dreams versus Process

People who lack *process* or the *sufficient use of process* are often known as dreamers.

Don't misunderstand me. I'm not against dreams, having dreams, or being a dreamer. After all, every great achievement began with a dream. And it doesn't matter if you're talking about Disney World, the space shuttle, the computer, or Google. Every great achievement starts with a dream. Someone dared to dream, to believe it was possible … and … And … *acted* on that dream.

Don't miss the emphasis on *acted*. Those who acted, with the right processes, have the power of *The Champion Edge* working for them.

It's like the cartoon I saw of two dinosaurs standing on the last bit of land sticking out of the water as the whole world was being covered by a flood in Noah's time. As they watched Noah's ark sailed away to safety, one dinosaur said to the other, "Oh crap, was that today??" Without process, the ship sails on and the dreamer is left behind.

So yes, you should have a noble *purpose* and a fired-up *passion*—in other words, a dream—but without the *process* of action, you're not going too far.

Don't be misled by some new-age psychobabble that tells you the "secret" to success is simply dreaming about it. Nope! You also need a *process.* Don't be caught up in the romantic notion promulgated by the Everly Brothers classic song, "All You Have To Do Is Dream."

You remember the song. The lyrics went like this:

- *Drea-ea-ea-ea-eam, dream, dream, dream.*
- *Drea-ea-ea-ea-eam, dream, dream, dream.*
- *When I want you in my arms,*
- *When I want you and all your charms,*
- *Whenever I want you, all I have to do is*
- *Drea-ea-ea-ea-eam, dream, dream, dream.*

Great melody. A lot of fun to sing. But you'll get in trouble if you take the lyrics to heart and apply them to your career and life as a whole. A *purpose* gives you a reason to live and work; it gives you a destination. A *passion* keeps you headed in that direction. But without a *process* to get there, chances are you're not going to get there. You're not going to have the full *Champion Edge* working for you.

And if you don't know *what* processes you have to use, you can get mighty discouraged in the pursuit of your professional career or personal life goals. You may quit your job—in fact or in theory. (We all know people who have retired but haven't told the Personnel Department yet.) Or you may leave your dreams, friends, family, and everything else that is important to you, behind. That's the bad news.

As much as I hate to say it, I've got some other bad news for you. There isn't one, for-sure, guaranteed no-fail process that you can use on every challenge that crosses your path. There isn't one single process or step-by-step program that you can use for strategically planning the future of your company, building your team at work, selling more products to your customers, improving your marriage, bettering your health, and everything else you want.

However, and this is good news, I have discovered *three major processes* behind every champion. Somehow or other, the champion has consciously or unconsciously, deliberately, or accidentally, tapped into the power of one or more of these processes. It was the proper use of these processes that turned their purpose and passion into reality.

The even better news is these three processes are fairly quick, easy, and simple. That's encouraging because if you're like a lot of my customers, you may be thinking, "I don't care about the theory. Just tell me what I have to do to get the results I want."

Process Is Personal and Interpersonal

One of these processes is personal. It is something you need to do for yourself. You need the *process of affirming achievement* (see Chapter 11) so you accomplish more goals in less time with less effort.

Two of the processes are interpersonal things you have to do with others. You need to learn, practice, and implement the *process of connective communication* (see Chapter 12). Many of the goals you want to achieve on and off the job will require the willing cooperation of others. That cooperation starts with your communication competence and is completed by the *process of compassionate listening* (see Chapter 13).

As you move through these three processes, *please* don't read them and move on. Devour them. Use them. Practice them. Master them. Just knowing about them won't do you much good. In fact, they'll be as useless as a car without a steering wheel.

The Champion Edge makes it clear that the big payoffs in life or on the job come when you have all the elements of purpose, passion, *and* processes working for you. Let's dig into the three processes that will bring you the results you desire.

CHAPTER 11

The Process of Affirming Achievement

How Your Mind Got Stuck on the Wrong Program

Imagine that you're in a boat and the autopilot is set for east, but you decide you want to change directions and go west. You take hold of the wheel and using all your might, you force the boat west. As long as you hold the wheel steady, the boat keeps on going west. But pretty soon, you get tired of fighting the boat's inclination and let go of the wheel. And once again, you're heading east—because that's the direction the boat is programmed to go.

As John Baker notes in *Life's Healing Choices* (New York: Howard Books, 2013), "That's how it is when you try to fight against your own internal autopilot. By your own willpower, you try to force new behavior. You try and you try, but pretty soon you get tired . . . and you let go of the wheel . . . and you revert back to the way you've always acted."[1]

If you don't know *where* your autopilot is set, and if you don't know *how* to reset your autopilot for the results you want, you will revert to any one of a hundred nonproductive behaviors. That's why most people do not come close to reaching their full career and life potential. Their autopilot is stuck on the wrong setting.

And that may be of true of you as well. Your autopilot or mental programming may be the victim of the exposure–adoption–addiction cycle, and you didn't even know it.

When you were young, for example, you may have been *exposed* to the negative comments of others, thousands of times. You were told repeatedly such comments as "No, you can't do that." "You'll never amount to anything." "You never listen to me." "You're no good at math."

Unfortunately, this type of negative programming from others didn't stop when you left home, graduated from school, or became an adult.

When you got a job, your exposure to negative conditioning continued and sometimes accelerated. You were exposed to a variety of comments that implied other people didn't believe in you or your ideas. Author Jack Canfield calls them "killer statements" because they kill off your energy, your enthusiasm, your initiative, and your effectiveness if you don't know how to respond to them.

There are hundreds of killer statements that get in the way of you becoming the champion you want to become. I'm sure you can relate. You bring up an idea at work, and people respond to you by saying such things as: "We've never done that kind of thing before," "That wouldn't work here," "We tried that five years ago," "That's not my job," "We're too busy for that," or "You're right, but . . ."

After you've been exposed to enough negative feedback, you may unwittingly *adopt* a narrower, smaller, more limited outlook or mindset. In a sense, you throw up your mental arms or throw in the towel and get used to getting by instead of getting ahead. You allow your mental autopilot to be stuck on the wrong setting.

However, and this is critical, what people are saying out there—at home or on the job—is not nearly as important as what you're telling yourself. After you've adopted enough of the negatives, you can actually get *addicted* to that way of thinking and start telling yourself your own set of self-defeating negative comments. I call them "Mind Binders," and the more you think them or say them, the less successful you're going to be in your business career and life.

Again, there are lots of them. I'm sure you've heard people say some of the following, or maybe you tell yourself some of these Mind Binders:

- I can't remember people's names . . .
- I'll never understand accounting . . .
- I'll never get that promotion . . .
- I'm no good at giving presentations . . .
- I can't lose weight . . .
- I can't seem to save any money . . .
- I've got too much work to do . . .
- I'll never get caught up . . .
- I always get a headache at 3:00 p.m. . . . .

Mind Binders are absolutely disastrous because they keep your auto-pilot stuck on the wrong setting, preventing you from getting the results you want and need.

That's what happened to Karl Wallenda when he let the Mind Binders get to him. Back in the 1960s, the flying Wallendas were seen as the finest circus act in the world. They took the art of tightrope walking to the great extreme and the very dangerous. In fact, Karl Wallenda loved it so much, in 1968 he said, "Walking the tightrope is living. Everything else is working."[2]

His wife noted that never once in all his life, in his entire career, did Karl even think about falling. But in Puerto Rico, with his rope stretched between two skyscrapers, and with thousands of people watching, Karl fell to the pavement and his death.

His wife later said that for the last three months of his life, Karl had been consumed by one thought—"I'm going to fall." He never thought of it before, but now that was all he thought about.

Karl did not understand that worry is negative goal setting. He did not understand that you are drawn to the very thing that fills your mind. As Mrs. Wallenda later said, Karl put all his energy into falling rather than walking, and the minute he did that he was destined to fall.

The good news is you can reset your autopilot to achieve what you want to achieve.

Give Your Autopilot a Temporary Reset

Take a moment, once in a while, to check out your thoughts. Notice how often you're thinking negative thoughts about yourself, your life, your job, your relationships, or anything else. In fact, if you find yourself sinking, *pay attention to what you're thinking.* Be especially careful of thinking any of the four most common, self-defeating Mind Binders:

- I am not _____ (good, smart, attractive, etc.) enough.
- I am a victim of _____ (my past, my upbringing, my genes, my boss's whims, etc.).
- I cannot trust _____ (myself, my decisions, my opinions, my preferences, or whatever).

- I am not worthy of other people's _____ (love, respect, time, recognition, help, etc.).

These statements are all indications of an autopilot that will hurt you instead of help you. After all, your thoughts are not some innocent innocuous bystander in your life. Indeed, what you think about you tend to bring about. As author Florence Shinn (1871–1940) wrote, "The game of life is the game of boomerangs. Our thoughts, deeds, and words return to us sooner or later, with astounding accuracy."[3]

Use one or more of the following techniques to give your autopilot a temporary reset.

Refute Your Mind Binders

As soon as you think one of them or speak one of them, talk back to yourself. Tell yourself, firmly and authoritatively, to "Stop it. Now just stop it!" Or follow up any negative thought with a command that says, "Cancel. Cancel." With repetition, you neutralize the negative thoughts and reset your autopilot, at least for the moment.

Reject Your Mind Binders

Avoid the use of such words as "can't." As industrialist Henry Ford (1863–1947) put it, "Whether you think you can or think you can't, you're right."[4]

Eliminate the word "impossible" from your vocabulary. One of my students helped me do that when she gave me a poster that read, "An impossibility is nothing more than a big idea striking a small mind." And the business books and the sports pages are filled with stories of people who did the impossible because they refused to speak the word "impossible."

Reprimand Your Mind Binders

Just keep a rubber band on one of your wrists, and whenever you think a negative thought or utter a negative comment, snap the rubber band.

Sure, it will hurt a little, but it's a simple way to cut down on your old, negative, self-destructive thoughts and give your autopilot a temporary reset.

You give your autopilot a temporary reset when you use these techniques. Using the process of affirming achievement, you could also give your autopilot a *permanent* reset.

Give Your Autopilot a Permanent Reset

This is where you get the biggest returns—when you follow a proven process of setting and using affirmations, which are carefully crafted declarations of the goals you want and expect to achieve, and which are deployed through a step-by-step system.

Of course, affirmations are not new. They've been around a long time. You've probably heard of them, and you may even have tried them. But if you're like a lot of people, you didn't know the exact process to follow, and so your results were mixed, at best. That's why comedian Al Franken satirized affirmations for years on *Saturday Night Live*. Playing the character of Stuart Smalley, he was known for his signature ever-present affirmation, "I'm good enough; I'm smart enough, and doggone it, people like me."

When you follow the *process of affirming achievement*, you can permanently reset your autopilot to achieve amazing results. Indeed, my files are filled with testimonials from hundreds of my students. Such as Barbara who is a manager at the largest privately held company in the United States. She writes, "Using your affirmation techniques, I am eating well-balanced meals, losing weight, and have more energy than ever! I got a new job that pays a great deal better, and even applied your techniques to our family finances for a net gain of $125,000. As you can tell, I have made some very positive changes. Thanks!"

The process of affirming achievement works equally well in your business career and personal life. Marilyn, a graphic arts designer for a Fortune 100 company, said she was stuck in a rut of low self-esteem, had lost her ability to be assertive at work, and overall had lost her focus in life and work. But she said, "Your affirmation process changed all that. I started a weight-loss program and lost ten pounds. At work, I learned how to work with difficult people, when necessary, and I've made progress on projects that I didn't think I could do before. I am no longer letting the negative talk get into my head, and my positive attitude is coming back because of what you taught me. If I don't watch out, I might start humming out loud again!"

So how do you get the process of affirming achievement working for you? Here are four steps you can follow.

Affirmation Step #1: Define Your Goals

The process starts with clarity. If you aren't clear about your goals, you won't like the results you get.

To start the process of defining *your* goals, ask yourself the following questions.

What Do You Really, Really Want?

Start the process by brainstorming your wants and desires. Decide what you want—not what you think you want, or might want, or what someone else thinks you should want, but what *you* really want! Get out a piece of paper and write down *everything* you want, desire, wish, and hope for. The longer your list the more useful it will be.

Your wants might include improvements in certain areas of your life. You may want to improve your golf score or increase the number of sales you close. You may want to modify your behavior in certain situations. You may want to be more assertive with your coworkers or more open with your family members. You may want to change a personality characteristic or drop a bad habit.

How Much Balance Do You Have in Your List?

Once you've brainstormed your list of possible wants, make sure you've listed at least one or more wants in each of the eight dimensions of life: physical, recreational, financial, occupational, social, mental, emotional, and spiritual.

If you have one goal, such as making a million dollars in a year, and if you dedicated every bit of your time, energy, and thought into that one goal, the chances of you achieving that goal are pretty good. But chances are also good that your life, your health, your relationships, and everything else would be a mess. So a healthy, balanced, effective champion has some positive goals in each of the eight dimensions of life.

What Would You Want If You Knew You Could Not Fail?

Don't waste your time wondering whether your wants and desires are practical or possible. That's premature. In most cases, when you follow the process of affirming achievement, you will be able to acquire most, if not all, of the things you desire. So don't let fear hold you back from making your thorough list. Just write down everything you want.

What Do You Want to Subtract from Your Life?

Maybe you want to get rid of your procrastination, your disorganization, your inability to cope with certain people, or a bad habit such as the excess use of food, nicotine, and alcohol. Write them all down.

Thus far, everything you have written down probably falls into a "get" category. You want to get yourself financially stabilized, get that promotion at work, get your marriage on stronger footing, and get yourself in better shape. And that's great. You should have some "get" goals to work on.

What Are Your "Be" Goals?

Two, three, five, or ten years from now, you will be a different person. Have you figured out what you want that person to *be*? Or are you just drifting through life, thinking whatever happens happens?

A champion would never take that approach. A champion knows that goal setting and achieving involves a lot more than *getting* a bunch of stuff; it's also about *becoming* the right kind of person.

So you need to list everything you want to *be*. Close your eyes and imagine your ideal self, possessing all the qualities you would like to have. List eight to ten qualities that describe the kind of person you want to become in the future. Maybe you want to be more self-confident, be more skilled in selling your product, be more effective in managing your team, or be a bigger risk taker.

Affirmation Step #2: Write Your Goals as Affirmations

Once you've figured out goals you want to set, you need to write them down. The research is clear. If you're not willing to put your goals on paper, you probably won't achieve them. The act of writing shows your commitment and gives your mind a sense of direction. You're telling your subconscious mind that of all the millions of possibilities out there, these are the few you would like.

This is one of the most important, self-motivating practices of all time. Put all of your personal and professional goals in writing. And if you're not currently doing this, let me assure you it will literally change your life.

For example, I had a goal for 18 years to write a book, and that goal was buried deep in my subconscious. As a subconscious goal for 18 years, I did not write a single word. Once I put my goal in writing, it only took me two years to complete that first book. And I've written several books since then, all as a result of writing down my goals as affirmations.

Of course, some of you are whining. You'll tell me you're not the writing type. Or you don't have the time to write out your goals. Well maybe, just maybe, that's why you haven't achieved all you are capable of achieving. As Sir Francis Bacon (1561–1626) advised, "If we are to achieve results never before accomplished, we must employ methods never before attempted."[5]

Think about it. If you're a manager who wants to ensure an employee's follow-through, you might ask him to write down your instructions. If you're giving directions over the phone, you might ask the other person to read back what she has written. You wouldn't let the other person off the hook without making sure they got the message. So why would you let yourself off the hook by not writing out your goals as affirmations?

This is a critical part of the process of affirming achievement. Your mind responds to certain language structures. If you don't write your affirmations *correctly*, they won't work the wonders you want. So please do the following as you write out your affirmations.

Use a Present Tense Verb in Your Affirmations

Say, "I am filled with energy and vitality," rather than "I will be energetic." And say, "I am confident in my telephone sales," rather than "I will be confident." Your mind will do its best to fulfill a present verb statement, but it will ignore future "will" statements.

Use the Word "I"

Personalize your affirmations. Write something like, "I am the top sales person in my region," or "I weigh a slim, trim 150 pounds." Remember, affirmations are used for *your* goal accomplishment, not somebody else's. You can't have an affirmation for somebody else. You can't say, "My employees will become more accountable" and expect it to work. Affirmations focus on what *you* are going to do.

State Your Affirmations Positively

Avoid words like *no, not,* or *never.* Write down what you want instead of what you don't want. Rather than telling yourself, "I don't fail any of my MBA exams," say, "I pass each of my MBA tests with high scores." It simply works a great deal better to focus on what you're going to do instead of what you're not going to do. At the same time, avoid *overly* positive sentences such as "I can lose forty pounds in two weeks." It would be more appropriate to say something like "I am achieving my ideal weight by controlling my eating habits and improving my exercise program."

It's a matter of focus. Your mind and behavior move toward your focus. When I told myself, "I won't get nervous when I'm making cold calls to prospective customers," guess what I focused on? Getting nervous, speaking ineffectively, and saying some stupid things. And that's exactly what I did.

However, when I changed my affirmation and focus to the positive, my mind and behavior followed along. Now I tell myself, "I speak with confidence and communicate clearly when I'm talking to prospective customers." Again, that's exactly what happens. So state your affirmations positively.

Be Specific

Your mind does not relate to vague goals or generalized hopes. If you want to improve your memory, you might say, "I have an excellent memory with clear and easy recall." That's specific. If you want to earn more money, tell yourself, "I am earning $_____ this year," and fill in the exact amount you want to make. That works a whole lot better than telling yourself, "I'm making more money."

The more specific your affirmations, the quicker you will reach your goal. Specificity gives you focus. It clarifies the target. It points you toward the bull's eye. There's an old saying, "When a ship misses the harbor, it is seldom the harbor's fault." And when your mind fails to achieve a goal, it is seldom your mind's fault. It's the vagueness of your target that causes the problem.

Use Words with Feeling

Even though you may not initially believe your affirmations will work, say them like you mean it. Better yet, put a feeling word into the affirmation itself. There's more power in an affirmation that says, "I am eagerly preparing and calmly delivering presentations at work" than "I am preparing and delivering presentations at work." Adding feeling words like "eagerly" and "calmly" makes a huge, motivating difference.

Affirmation Step #3: Deploy Your Affirmations

Once you've consciously written your affirmations, you need to move them into your subconscious. Because that's where your negative autopilot or your negative mental programming resides. So you want to make sure you've got your subconscious working for you and not against you. To move your affirmations into your subconscious, use the following process.

Relax

Let your body relax because tension blocks the information flow between the conscious and subconscious levels of thought. You might try sitting up straight in a comfortable chair, placing your feet flat on the floor, resting your hands on your lap, and closing your eyes. If you simply don't have the time or the place to be that relaxed, say them anyway—in the shower, walking the dog, or driving to work. And by the way, if you say them in the car on the way to work, I suggest keeping your eyes open.

Repeat

The best way to move your affirmations into your subconscious is through repetition. Repeat your affirmations to yourself over and over again. Say each one of them four or five times, either silently or out loud, during three different times throughout your day. For most people it works best if you say them the first thing in the morning, sometime around lunch for midday correction, and as the last thing before you go to bed.

Don't skip this step. It's absolutely critical that you be persistent in saying your affirmations if they are to work.

Review

After you've said your affirmations, take a few seconds to *view* them or visualize each of them. Just imagine each of them as having come true. There is a strange but powerful force that works to create what you affirm and what you imagine.

If you're not used to visualizing, try this. Visualize each of your affirmations for 10 seconds each. Vividly imagine yourself in situations where you are acting out, practicing, and/or living the affirmation. *See* yourself closing that sale, inspiring your staff, working out for 30 minutes each day, or whatever achievements your affirmations indicate.

All goals are mind accomplished before they are materially accomplished. If you can't see yourself as a successful businessperson, you may never become one. If you can't see yourself speaking more persuasively to potential investors, you probably won't. But if you can *see* yourself doing, having, or being your affirmations, you will be taking a major step toward their accomplishment.

Remember

You've heard the conventional wisdom that it takes 21 days to form a new habit such as saying your affirmations every day and then getting the accomplishment you want. That's bunk. Scientists who study habit formation say there isn't a magic number—and even if there was, it would be more like 66 days, according to one recent study led by University College London research psychologist Phillippa Lally. For some people, she says new healthy habits can be established in a mere 18 days—while others may take as long as 254 days.[6]

The point is, you must *remember* to declare your affirmations until you no longer need them. Until you've achieved *The Champion Edge* results you're looking for. You probably won't make a million dollars or lose 100 pounds in those mythical 21 days. But if you're saying your affirmations every day, it does mean you're on the right path, doing the right things, and getting closer to your goals. Some affirmations take longer, but they still work. It took me two years of affirmations to overcome the pain and immobility of rheumatoid arthritis, and it took me five years to be ranked among the top five percent of all speakers worldwide.

Affirmation Step #4: Ensure the Success of Your Affirmations

As I mentioned earlier, many people have heard of affirmations and tried them—without all the success they were hoping for. That's because they messed up the process. To ensure the success of your affirmations, there are two "do's" and two "don'ts" you must follow.

Do Establish Some Triggers

You may think you don't have time to say your affirmations, or you may forget to do them. Well, you can't skip them or forget them and expect to succeed. Fortunately, there's a way to do them where you never forget and it takes no time whatsoever.

Establish triggers or little reminder events. When those events occur, you will remember to do your affirmations. A trigger may be your morning shower, your commute to work, waiting for your computer to boot up, or walking to lunch. Every time you do those activities, you will know it is your time to say your affirmations.

Do Make Sure Your Affirmations Are Physically Possible

I could write a well-written affirmation that declares, "I am the next King of England." It fits all the guidelines I gave you earlier, but it's never going to happen. I'm not in the royal family, and there's no chance of me inheriting the throne. It's not physically possible for me to achieve that affirmation. Don't forget: I'm teaching you a method, not a miracle. Your affirmations must be *physically possible.*

Don't Share Them with Dream Spoilers

Some people write their affirmations and post them on their bathroom mirror or near their computer screen. That's okay, *if* you live with and work with positive people. But if you're around folks who say, "What is this silly garbage . . . that you are the company's top performer? You're never going to make it," then keep them private. Or if someone says, "Your affirmation, how ridiculous, that you are an upbeat and optimistic person. You're the biggest grouch I know." Again, keep them private if you're around dream spoilers. They will discourage you from using the affirmation process.

However, if you work or live with positive, supportive people, feel free to post your affirmations where you can see them and be reminded of them. My staff members, for example, use their affirmations as screen savers so, whenever they step away from their computers and come back again, they can review their affirmations consciously or subliminally. It works in our office because everyone I hire is not only highly competent but also extremely positive, supporting one another in whatever has to be done.

Don't Be Fooled by Progress

This is by far the biggest way people mess up the process, and as a result, go around telling people, "I knew these affirmations wouldn't work."

They were fooled by progress. They wrote out their affirmations and began to say their affirmations, day after day, making some progress. They closed a few more sales, improved their customer service a little bit, got along better with their families, or ate a few less junk-food snacks. They weren't anywhere near the completion of their goal or affirmation, but they made progress, felt better, and no longer craved the goal quite so much.

That's exactly where most people *stop* saying their affirmations. And what happens? They always go back to start. That's why people have to start and restart diets, exercise programs, and every other change initiative over and over again. They were fooled by progress and failed to keep on saying their affirmations all the way through to the completion of the payoffs they were seeking.

But let's get more specific. If you adopt the process of affirming achievement, you can expect three champion outcomes.

Affirmation Outcome #1: Focus

As American novelist, Chuck Palahniuk puts it, "If you don't know what you want, you end up with a lot you don't."[8]

Sister Esther Boor taught me that as well. Through marriage I was related to her and had the privilege to visit with her and learn from her on a few occasions. Sister Esther died at the age of 107, and she'd been very alert and mobile her entire life. In fact, Sister Esther didn't retire from her teaching position until she was 98. After that, she only taught occasionally. Later, she and her fellow nuns were featured in *Time* magazine as a study of Catholic nuns who were living well into their nineties and hundreds.[9]

So I wondered, "What do these vigorous old nuns have to teach us?" When interviewed by *Time* magazine, almost every one of them said, "Plan your life. Set your goals." Or putting it in my terms, "Get focused." Affirmations will do that for you.

On one level, you already know the importance of focus. If you're a businessperson, you would never think of creating a business without a plan. And the really smart businesspeople would create an organized plan for the next 6, 12, and 18 months as well as a long-term plan. They would establish some benchmarks and bring in some consultants to show them the best way to reach their goals.

On another level, when you're decorating your house, you also understand the importance of focus. You don't throw a bunch of furniture into a room and hope it looks good. No, you think about where people will sit, where the best lighting is, and where the most convenient place for the TV is.

When you have thoughtfully considered and clearly written affirmations, you get focused. And that will bring you more of the results you want.

Affirmation Outcome #2: Motivation

If you're somewhat lacking in the energy, passion, attitude, and motivation departments, I know you're also lacking in the area of goal setting. There's no reason to be pumped up if you're not going anywhere in particular.

However, when you have exciting goals and affirmations, all sorts of powers are released within you. Inertia and procrastination are thrown out the window.

Perhaps you can relate. You may have a tough time getting out of bed in the morning. You push the snooze button on your alarm clock two or three times, and you slowly, reluctantly get yourself ready and off to work. After all, you figure, yesterday wasn't too exciting at work and today doesn't promise to be any better.

But let's say, instead, you get an early morning phone call. You're told by a reputable source that you've just won a trip to Hawaii and a half million dollars—provided you can be on the plane in three hours.

I suspect that new exciting goal would motivate you to achieve more that morning than you've achieved in the past 30 mornings put together. You would find places to send the kids and take the dog, and you would find people to fill in for you at work. You would be flying high instead of griping about your busy schedule or the drudgery of "another day another dollar."

Affirmation Outcome #3: Achievement

Better yet, with the right goals and affirmations, you will achieve more! I've seen it firsthand hundreds of times as I speak to audiences around the world. I know that goal setters who use the process of affirming achievement accomplish a great deal more than non-goal setters. They make more money, have better jobs, and build stronger families.

For example, you will achieve a great deal more if you affirm, "I am taking a seminar on dealing with difficult people, and I am improving my skills when I'm talking to them." You will achieve more with affirmations than you ever will with a Mind Binder such as "I'll never be able to handle those difficult coworkers."

Affirmations Bridge the Gap

One thing is certain. If you don't have and don't use affirmations, you'll end up somewhere you don't want to be.

Are you willing to do that? Are you willing to let your future be determined by chance or circumstance? Or do you want the ability to shape your future and make your dreams come true?

As a champion, you will choose the latter. And as you properly construct and use your affirmations, you will close the gap between where you are and where you want to be. That's *The Champion Edge* showing up in your life and career.

CHAPTER 12

The Process of Connective Communication

A Failure to Communicate

Almost everywhere I go to speak or consult, the employee surveys say the same thing. The employees say there is a "lack of communication."

In his book, *The Practice of Empowerment* (Brookfield, VT: Gower, 1995), Dennis C. Kinlaw documents this. He asked 1,000 people, "If you knew that a supervisor in your organization was doing something that was hurting the performance of the organization, would you confront that person about what he or she was doing?" Less than 50 percent of respondents said they would talk to or communicate with their bosses about the situation.

Kinlaw then asked another 6,000 people two additional questions. He asked, "Do you know of some way that your organization could make a substantial gain in cutting costs or improving the quality of its goods and services?"[1] Almost 100 percent of the people answered "yes." And then he asked, "Will you do anything about it?" Fewer than 10 percent said they would bring up their idea and talk about it. Obviously, there is a failure to communicate in lots of places.

Perhaps you work or live in one of those places. You may even be discouraged or depressed about the lack of communication or the ineffectiveness of that communication. I've got some good news for you: communication works for those who work at it—intelligently. Champions have mastered this process, and so can you.

The *process of connective communication* comes down to avoiding *communication busters* and using *communication builders* instead.

In essence, a *communication buster* is anything you say or do that pushes people away from you emotionally. It sends the message that I don't respect you, understand you, and/or care about you. As a result, people are less open with you, trusting you less and liking you less. And these busters will absolutely kill off your effectiveness with people.

A *communication builder* sends a different message. It's anything you say or do with other people—in person, over the phone, in writing, or electronically—that says, "You count. You matter. You're worthy of my time and attention. And I will do my best to make sure we understand each other." You may send that message directly or imply it indirectly, but the message is there nonetheless.

From my experience, champions are invariably great communicators. They avoid the *communication busters* you are about to discover and they apply the upcoming *communication builders* to all their relationships. Let me offer one caveat, however. I have several degrees in communication, and I know there is no way that one chapter in a book could cover everything there is to know about communication. But I also know you will make quick and dramatic improvements in your communication effectiveness when you follow these tips. Use them. They add extra power to *The Champion Edge* you are developing.

Communication Buster #1: Superficiality

In many relationships, communication is superficial at best. Conversation is reduced to the closing numbers of yesterday's stock market, the road conditions on the way to work, the weather outside, and how a certain football team is doing.

When you keep things superficial, share too little of yourself, or keep too many things light, glossed over or hidden, your personal relationships are in jeopardy. According to research by marriage expert Dr. Gary D. Chapman, 85 percent of failed relationships show a lack of communication.[2] The people kept too much inside, and so they grew apart.

The same thing is true of your professional relationships. They don't work when information is hoarded or the people do not share what they know, think, and feel—directly with one another. If you find your coworkers saying one thing in a staff meeting and something else outside in the hallway after the meeting, you've got a communication problem that needs to be fixed ASAP.

The only way you can get the best ideas and make the best decisions in any relationship or work team is to get beyond the superficiality. To share more of your thoughts, feelings, joys, and concerns. As the Swedish proverb reminds us, "Shared joy is a double joy. Shared sorrow is half a sorrow." In fact, that's one of the secrets of teamwork.

Communication Buster #2: Blabbering

Blabbering comes in two varieties.

First, communication busts up when a *person talks too much, in general.* I'm sure you know people who just talk on, and on, and on. I don't know what's driving their behavior. But I do know they're usually driving other people nuts.

You've probably had the experience of working with colleagues who don't know when to shut up. They talk incessantly about anything and everything. It may not be their intention, but their incessant talking sends the message that they are more interested in hearing themselves talk than in connecting with you. And as a result, you probably find yourself avoiding those colleagues.

To get beyond blabbering, *make sure you have something worthwhile to say before you say it.* Before you speak, ask yourself a few questions: "Do others want to hear what I have to say? Are my comments worth saying?"

As the great philosopher Plato said thousands of years ago, "Wise men talk because they have something to say; fools, because they have to say something." Good advice for all of us. Let's make sure we take it.

You also need to *remember the privilege of the platform.* Every time you speak, you are using up someone else's time. And considering the precious nature of time, it's quite an honor when people tune into you. So don't waste too much of their time blabbering on about the trite and irrelevant.

The late great actor Charlton Heston took that privilege seriously. One of my colleagues learned that when he was seated next to Charlton Heston on a plane. As they talked, Heston mentioned he was coming from a conference where he had addressed 112 people. Of course, my colleague thought how disappointing that must have been for Heston, being a world-famous actor, when only a few people came to his presentation. Nonetheless, my colleague knew Heston was also a world-class communicator, so he asked him what the secret to his powerful communication ability was.

Heston replied, "I have never gotten over the miracle that someone will come to listen to me speak." He held the communication process in such high regard that he made sure he never abused the process.

Second, communication busts up when *people talk too much about themselves.* They bring every point made at a staff meeting back to them. And they turn every story shared at a party into an opportunity to say, "that reminds me of," which sends them into a lengthy monologue. In essence, they're sending the message, "I'm so important and I'm so interesting that you simply must know this about me." As David L. Levin points out in his book, *Don't Just Talk, Be Heard!* (Minneapolis, MN: Minneapolis Press, 2009), "Anything that says me, me, me is a disconnect."[3] It breaks up communication.

Author Les Giblin writes, "When you talk to people about yourself, you are rubbing people the wrong way and working against human nature. Take these four words out of your vocabulary—I, me, my, mine. Substitute for those four words, one word, the most powerful word spoken by the human tongue—you."[4]

Of course, Giblin is exaggerating a bit to make his point, but his point is well taken. If *you* will give up the satisfaction *you* get from talking about *yourself* too much, if *you* relinquish some of the attention *you* get from the use of the words "I, me, my, and mine," *your* personality, influence, and communication will be greatly enhanced.

Communication Buster #3: Discounting

Most people aren't consciously rude or deliberately hurtful, but they may do it anyway. They say something or do something that discounts another person. And their communication devalues or cheapens the people around them, saying in effect, "You don't count."

Of course, you may think this buster does not apply to you. You don't discount others. I hope that's the case. But you may discount others without even knowing it. You may use some communication behaviors that seem natural or inconsequential to you, but they may have a huge negative impact on other people and your relationships with them.

Failing to Acknowledge Others

You discount others when you fail to acknowledge them. It happens all too often. You're in a store, waiting to be waited on, while the clerk keeps talking to her friend on the phone. And even though she sees you, she refuses to stop her conversation or even nod in your direction. It's a communication buster. Whether she means to or not, she is communicating "I don't respect you enough to even acknowledge your existence."

The same principle applies to your internal customers. I'm sure you've seen managers and vice-presidents chatting among themselves, while the underlings wait to be acknowledged or included. It's not cool. It's a communication buster. You're discounting others.

So make sure you acknowledge people when they come into sight, whether it's nodding in their direction, saying "Hi" to a coworker who passes by in the hallway, or asking a question. It communicates caring and some respect.

Interrupting Others

You discount others when you interrupt them. As David L. Levin goes on to say, consider the message it sends. When you interrupt others, you're saying, in effect, "I'm much more interested in what I'm going to say next than in what you're saying to me right now."[5] It's a biggie in the world of discounting others. So for heaven's sake, watch yourself; catch yourself, and stop interrupting people.

Gossiping about Others

You discount others when you gossip about them. It's not always easy to do this. There's something very alluring and maybe even a little satisfying, about sharing a negative tidbit. It may make you feel a bit superior, but you've got to fight the urge to bash others or add to the gossip that other people are sharing. You just can't do it, if you ever want to build trust with the person you are discussing. The real art of communication and trust is not only saying the right thing at the right time, but it's also stopping yourself from saying the wrong thing at the most tempting moment.

I had to learn that the hard way when I was working my way through college as a shoe salesman. One day, two very attractive young women entered the store, and I immediately rushed over to be the one who waited on them. As we chatted and flirted, one of the young women picked up a pair of women's black, old-fashioned, high top, lace-up shoes that looked a bit like army combat boots. She said, "I wouldn't be caught dead in a pair of shoes like this. Does anyone actually wear such ugly monstrosities?"

To be cute, I replied, "The only person I know who wears shoes like that is old lady Sampson, and I'm not even sure she's alive." The young women laughed a bit, and I thought, "Great! I've charmed them a bit. I'm making progress."

At that same moment, I turned and there stood Dr. Sampson, my English literature teacher, a dear sweet soul, about 75 years old. She had just watched and heard my utterly disrespectful gossip. She smiled and said, "Good morning, Alan. I look forward to seeing you in class tomorrow." I had to learn once again— and maybe you have too—that gossip is not the way to building better relationships.

The strange thing is we live in the information technology age where we have never been more connected—but less engaged. All too many people, as well as their companies and relationships are limping along, failing to reach their potential, because they do not know how to communicate. The *communication builders* will turn that around for you. Use them.

Communication Builder #1: Take More Time to Talk

Some people just don't take enough time to talk to the other people in their lives. As clinical psychologist Dr. Dana Fillmore says, "The average couple can spend as little as one hour alone together per week; the average couple with kids—sometimes none." There is very little communication going on.

In a survey of 2,000 parents by Virgin Holidays and Universal Orlando Resort that was reported in the *Daily Mail*, the average family spends less than 30 minutes of meaningful time together each day as work schedules, chores, and school routines divert their attention. Even when they are together, seven in ten parents say the time is spent sitting in silence in front of the television, reading, or playing computer games instead of talking to one another.[6]

Without even realizing it, many people take their personal relationships for granted and then wonder why there is a problem. I tell those people, "Don't fool yourself. Don't sacrifice your family for the sake of your job, because no success in business will ever make up for a failure at home." I know. I made that mistake one time, and it took me years to rectify the damage.

I teach them the Big Truck theory. The Big Truck theory says, "If you get hit and killed by a big truck today, someone else will be doing your job tomorrow. But if you get hit and killed today, you will never be replaced at home. You will be missed forever."

Now that might sound soft and sappy coming from me—a person whose entire career is focused on leadership, motivation, and teamwork programs for business, government, education, and health care groups. But I've learned that it's very difficult for me or anyone else to exert inspirational leadership, disperse meaningful motivation, and build effective teamwork if your home life is a mess.

And the world of work is just as challenging when it comes to communication time. One of the most frequent complaints I hear from my clients is "We're so busy we don't even have time to talk to each other. We're so focused on our own individual silos that we don't really know the other people in our company or understand what they're doing."

If that sounds anything like you, then I urge you to start scheduling some communication time with the important others in your life and work. And yes, I know that sounds cold and mechanical, but in our crazy busy world, I've learned if it's not on the calendar it doesn't happen.

So schedule your 10, 20, 30-minute get-togethers, if necessary. Don't leave it to chance. Don't wait until you're free from other obligations. It will never happen. That's why my wife actually put a time on our calendar to talk about our marriage, our feelings, hopes, dreams, goals, and frustrations.

You've got to put it on your calendar. And nothing short of an emergency should change that schedule. Skipping your scheduled communication times sends the message that you don't care that much. Keeping your commitment affirms the value of your relationship and affirms each person in the relationship.

You've also got to meet with some degree of frequency. For people at work, it might be once a month. For people at home, it might be every week. Do not save your scheduled communication times until you've got some serious issues to discuss. If you wait until the stress and pressures are at the boiling point, you'll be trying to communicate without any of the relationship-building ground work being done in advance.

Indeed, I would rank scheduled times to talk among the top five things that have brought *The Champion Edge* to my career. For 20 years, I have been meeting with nine super successful businesspeople that would be household names for many of you. We schedule four meetings a year, that last two days each in length, to simply talk about our successes and failures, our ideas and dreams, giving advice to one another and listening intently. We are absolutely committed to this time and each other, scheduling the meetings one year in advance, with the only acceptable excuse for non-attendance is a family emergency. These communication meetings have literally given me dozens of ideas that helped me build a solid financial structure on which to operate my professional career—ideas that I would not have accessed any other way.

Communication Builder #2: Encourage Openness

This is a biggie. It's one of the most important characteristics of quality communication. Everyone in a champion organization, on a team, or in a family is encouraged to share what he or she really thinks, feels, knows, and wants—which may or may not be politically correct or what the other person wants to hear.

Throughout my career, however, I've come across many managers and leaders who say, "My people just don't speak up. I ask for their input, but they don't say much to me or at out our meetings. So I suppose we're all pretty much in synch."

No, that may not at all be the case. But there are certain things you can do that actually encourages the other person to be more open with you.

Select a Mutually Acceptable Place to Talk

Each person needs to enter the discussion with a sense of ease instead of fear. And choosing a mutually agreed-upon place to meet is a good start. You may want to avoid places that are the obvious turf of one party or the other. And you may want to choose a location that offers a degree of privacy, where no one else is observing you or listening in. The very fact that you will be sharing your thoughts and feelings and that you will be giving feedback to one another suggests some degree of privacy.

Create a Safe Communication Environment

Everyone needs to know that they're entering a discussion that will be somewhat friendly and respectful instead of hostile. Creating rules of engagement, in advance, will do that for you. You may decide, for example, that you each have the right to talk and to be heard, but not necessarily agreed with. Your rules may outlaw all rudeness, sarcasm, put-downs, and name-calling, no matter how upset someone might get. And you may establish a rule of confidentiality—that after the discussion there will be no sharing of the discussion with other team members or whomever. You get the idea. Draw up and write down your rules of engagement.

Adopt a Mindset that Welcomes Openness

As silly as it may sound, people really can feel how open you are to their openness. It's not something you can fake. So get it through your head— or make a decision right now—that you truly *welcome* the input of others. After all, champion communicators know they can't think of everything. And they know they are much more apt to find the right answer to a problem if they have several possible solutions in front of them.

It's another characteristic of *The Champion Edge*. President John F. Kennedy certainly knew that. One of his close advisers said Kennedy tried to "surround himself with people who raised questions . . . and was wary of those who adapted their opinions to what they thought the president wanted to hear."

Facilitate the Other Person's Openness

Some people will quickly and easily share their input. Others need a little help to do that. Ask them specifically what they're thinking or how they're feeling. Some people wait for an invitation before they speak. It's just the way they're wired.

And when you ask for their input, refrain from superficial "yes" or "no" questions. Refrain from questions that ask something like "Are you okay with this?" The quiet people may give you a polite "Yes" or "Yeah, I'm okay." But that's a far cry from openness or sharing the whole truth.

Use behavioral descriptions followed by a question. For example, "I notice you haven't said anything during the meeting" or "I notice you looking down. What are you thinking about all of this?" You'll probably get a much more informative response.

Try the "one-word go-around." If you're having a team meeting or even a family discussion, go around the group and ask each person how he or she feels in one word. You'll often be surprised by their answers.

All of these techniques will increase the *quantity* of your communication. To increase the *quality* of your communication as well, do the following.

Communication Builder #3: Up the Trust Level

I give my coaching clients a slogan that may appear to be a little silly, but I'm dead serious. And that is *trust is must or the relationship will bust*. In other words, No Trust = No Communication. Know Trust = Honest Communication. You can up that trust level with these strategies.

Reward the other person's contribution

When someone shares a thought or an idea, make sure you *respond* to it. Say something like "Thanks for sharing" or "It's good to know where you stand." You're not saying you agree with what was said; you just appreciate the fact the other person contributed to the discussion. If you give no response, the other person feels overexposed or violated and will trust even less in the future.

The same principle applies when someone shares a feeling. Make sure you *honor* that feeling. Respond with something like "Of course you're feeling confused. Who wouldn't be in this situation?" Or "Your frustration certainly makes sense." Again, you're not saying her feeling is right or wrong; you are simply acknowledging the feeling.

Look for the good and comment on the good you see in others

According to psychologist Dr. John Gottman, this is a huge trust builder. After 30 years of research, Gottman concluded that when a couple's comments approach five positives for every negative, they *will* have a successful relationship. As your ratio approaches one positive for every negative, however, your chances of the relationship ending are fairly certain.[7]

Dr. Ken Blanchard, the author of *The One Minute Manager* (New York: William Morrow, 1982), reported similar results in the world of work. In one corporate study where positive and negative comments were actually tabulated and the reactions measured, where there was one criticism for each praising, the employees felt as though they had a totally negative relationship with the boss. When the ratio was changed to two praisings for each reprimand, people still thought their boss was all over them. It wasn't until they got to four praisings for each criticism that people began to feel as though they had a good relationship with their boss.[8]

Help people get to know others beyond their clique

One of my graduate students, Scott, a school principal in Wisconsin, knew that his teachers and staff did not know each other very well. Most of them stuck with their own little cliques in their own grade level or their own area of service. And the result was more suspicion than trust. So he put people in groups with people they did not know as well and gave them some of my "Brave Questions" (discussed at length in my book *Brave Questions: Building Stronger Relationships by Asking All the Right Questions* [Peak Performance Publications, 2012]) to ask one another.

As Scott said, even though a number of the staff was quite reluctant at first, the results were extremely positive. "We built new levels of friendship, trust, and understanding among one another, and I learned what made my staff tick."

Discuss your trust level

Debra Boggan, author of *Confessions of an Unmanager* (Richmond, VA: The Oaklea Press, 2004), said this technique made a huge and positive difference in her organization. She found that the supervisors were giving lip service to the new empowerment program, but they weren't really using it.

When she asked them about their commitment to the program, they all said they were behind it 100 percent. When she asked them how honest they'd just been in answering her question, they all avoided the question. She concluded that her team had a trust and communication problem.

So she asked her team members, "Do you trust everybody else in this room?" She asked them to anonymously write out their answers on a slip of paper. Everyone wrote, "No."

Fortunately, Boggan was a champion communicator. She knew her team couldn't make any progress as long as they had a lack of trust and an unwillingness to communicate. So she offered to put herself on the chopping block. She said, "Let's start with me. Why don't you trust me? And how exactly can I be better at my job?"

For the next couple of hours, her staff gave feedback. One said she wasn't a good listener, that she seemed so preoccupied with her own ideas that she shut out the ideas of others. Another one pointed out that when they were talking one to one, she would take phone calls or speed-read her e-mail. Still others said she gave mixed signals—that sometimes she wanted the team members to take initiative and other times she wanted to run everything.

As the session progressed, an important shift came when a supervisor said, "I give mixed signals too." Then others looked at how they could improve.[9]

Boggan knew that great leaders create a climate where their teammates speak up, share their ideas, and question the leader's point of view. She had taken the first step in making sure that would happen in her organization. She upped the trust level and opened up the floodgates to more honest communication.

It's Time to Get Past a Failure to Communicate

Miscommunication can be funny. In the women's fashion store where I worked as a salesman years ago, one of their window displays had a large sign that announced, "Bras half off." That got a lot of snickers from passersby on the street. And in one health care organization where I was speaking, they showed me their new marketing slogan. It read, "If you're at death's door, let our doctors pull you through." I suggested they not use the ad.

Yes, miscommunication can be funny. It's the very essence of what most comedians and television sitcoms do. But in your world, on the job or at home, a failure to communicate is an inefficient use of your time; at worst it destroys your relationships if not your business. Anything less than clear, open, honest, caring, and respectful communication will hurt you, not help you.

By contrast, anything you do that communicates the following message gives you more of *The Champion Edge*: "You count. You matter. You're worthy of my time and attention. Let's talk."

CHAPTER 13

The Process of Compassionate Listening

Talking Is Sharing but Listening Is Caring

I was invited to a wedding along with my 83-year-old grandmother. It was a two-hour drive that I wasn't looking forward to. Nonetheless, I decided to make the best of it. I had just learned about brave questions from professor emeritus Dr. Sidney Simon and decided I could at least practice the technique.

As Simon taught me, brave questions are deeper, more personal questions that get away from the superficiality of "How are you?" and "How about that football team?" They take guts to ask and guts to answer. Mixed with the process of compassionate listening, however, they can transform relationships.

Of course, it was a risk for me to initiate the process. Our entire relationship of some 30 or 40 years had consisted of nothing more than superficial conversation. We'd talk about the crafts she was making or what she was doing at the senior citizens' center, but we never talked about what she thought, how she felt, or what really counted in life.

So as nonchalantly as possible, I told grandma we had a long drive ahead of us, and I asked if she would be open to a little discussion exercise I had learned. "You can ask me anything at all, and I can ask you anything. Would that be okay?" She said that would be fine.

I started the process with a relatively easy question. I asked, "Grandma, you've lived a long time. What was the happiest moment of your life?"

She responded, saying she didn't know the happiest moment but she could think of the most blessed moment. Would that be okay? "Absolutely," I replied.

She went on to tell me that when she was 16, she was single and got pregnant. It stunned me. While it's not acceptable to be 16, single, and pregnant today, I could only imagine how awful that must have been some 80 or 90 years before in a small, conservative, Midwest farm town. I continued listening, using the best and most supportive listening skills I could muster.

Grandma continued, telling me that her parents had disowned her. She had nowhere to go. But a nearby farmer said she could stay in a room attached to his barn. The night she was giving birth, she was crying, feeling full of shame and remorse, and saying her whole life was ruined.

The midwife who came over to help her that night said, "I don't see it that way. You could have left town, tried to abort, or cover your tracks so no one could have put you down. But you did what you thought was right—to give birth to this child. And for that, I respect you."

I was stunned. I thought my first question for grandma was an easy one that would bring a light answer. I was wrong. Our conversation went on and on as we continued our drive to the wedding.

A bit further into the drive, referring to her pregnancy, I simply said, "Grandma, help me understand." (You'll learn more about this powerful statement question later in this chapter.) Grandma went on to explain that when she got pregnant, she wasn't doing anything wrong. In fact, she had never even had a date her entire life. Her only social event was a community dance when she turned 16.

Tragically, on the way home from that dance, she was raped. She tried to push the man away, but she couldn't do it. She had no recourse, because in those days, she said, people thought, "Boys will be boys," and if a woman got raped, "She was asking for it."

I was surprised and saddened. She had been carrying her secret burden for decades. But the *process of compassionate listening* made her feel safe enough to open up, and it put a depth into our relationship that we had never had before.

Let me tell you, there's power in this process. It dramatically improved my relationship with my grandma and every one of my personal and business relationships since then.

So how can you get this *Champion Edge* power working for you? Follow these listening skills and you'll soon be seeing better results with the people in your life and career.

Listening Skill #1: Acknowledge the Listening Problem

As you well know, you can't fix anything that isn't broken. Indeed, you have little or no motivation to even try and improve it. Well, listening falls into that category—of being an unacknowledged problem. If you can't get past this first point, you won't even bother with the rest of the listening skills in this chapter.

However, I'm going to give you the benefit of the doubt. I believe you want *The Champion Edge* working for you, which includes working effectively with others, and that always includes effective listening.

To put Listening Skill #1 to work for you, you need to acknowledge there *is* a problem in listening, on both a *general* and a *personal* level.

On a *general* level, research shows that the average person only listens to or remembers about 25 percent of what is being said.[1] And yet people seem to be oblivious to this fact. A study of over 8,000 people employed in businesses, hospitals, universities, the military, and government agencies found that virtually all of the respondents believed that they listen as effectively or more effectively than their coworkers.[2] That's crazy. There's no way that almost everyone could be above average.

To make matters worse, in a survey by the research firm Watson Wyatt Worldwide, they found that only 19 percent of managers say they listen to and take into account the comments of their employees before they make policies. Apparently, the higher people go in their careers and the more authority they wield, the less they are "forced" to listen to others. Indeed, the less they listen at all.

And that's dangerous. As you move up in your career, the *more* you should listen. After all, the farther you get from the front line, the *more* you have to depend on others for information.

So, in a *general* sense, would you acknowledge there *is* problem in listening? If so, great. That's the first step in becoming a better listener.

On a *personal* level, there are literally dozens of signs that someone has a listening problem. Here are just a few of them. If you can say yes to any of these behaviors, you have room for improvement.

- I find myself distracted by other things when I am supposed to listen to someone.

- If someone is difficult to understand, boring or uninteresting, I tend to tune them out.
- I have a hard time listening to speakers with whom I disagree.
- I find myself anticipating what a speaker is going to say, rather than listening to what is being said.
- I interrupt people before they have a chance to finish what they are saying.
- I find myself faking attention to a speaker while I am actually thinking of other things not related to what the speaker is saying.
- I have difficulty concentrating on what people are saying.
- I sometimes try to do two or more things at once, such as listening to a customer while completing some paperwork.
- I have a tendency to daydream at meetings, especially so after having made my statements or completed my presentation.

The problem is exacerbated when you figure you don't have to listen all that well because you already understand what the other person is saying or about to say. You assume understanding. But more often than not, when you and another person automatically *assume* you understand one another, as the word spells—a-s-s-u-m-e—you make an ass of you and me.

No matter how good the other person's communication skills might be—no matter how good you think your listening skills are—the message is seldom, if ever, perfectly understood by the parties involved. People simply see and hear things differently, all the time. So can you accept the fact, on a *personal* level, that you may need to improve your listening skills? If so, great. As I said above, that's the first step in becoming a better listener.

Listening Skill #2: Decide to Listen

When I ask my audience members, "How many of you can turn on your ability to listen if you need to or want to?" all the hands go up. Apparently, people have the ability to listen somewhat better, if and when they *decide* to do so. That decision includes the following.

Take Responsibility

You can't sit back and wait for someone's message to be dumped into your brain. You've got to take responsibility for getting the message. Ask yourself what you can do to get the most out of each and every listening experience. And then do it.

Over the years, I've had the opportunity to teach at universities and speak at conferences on four continents, and I've noticed huge cultural differences on this point of taking responsibility. In some cultures, they believe it's the *listener's job* and it's the *listener's responsibility* to get the message. In fact, 90 percent of the responsibility *is* in the listener's lap. No matter how good or bad a presenter or teacher might be, they've got to get the message! No excuses allowed.

In other cultures, I've noticed a very different expectation. They expect the speaker to give them the message—and be entertaining as well. They figure if a speaker or professor isn't that good at delivering the message, they don't have that much responsibility to listen. And I'm sure you can guess which culture ranks higher in academic achievement.

If you're going to be an excellent listener, you've got to take responsibility for getting the message. And that means, in part, to put aside your preoccupation with your present circumstances.

Don't Focus on Your Present Circumstances

In the midst of a conversation, you may be guilty of focusing on something going on in your life instead of what is being said at that very moment. I know I'm guilty of that some of the time. We get preoccupied with our present circumstances.

In fact, one New York columnist believed that was the case with a certain socialite who was so preoccupied with making an outstanding impression that she was unable to hear anything her guests were saying. To test his theory, he came late to her next party, and when he was greeted effusively at the door by the hostess, he said, "I'm sorry to be late, but I murdered my wife this evening and had the darndest time stuffing her body in the trunk of my car."

The super-charming hostess beamed and replied, "Well, darling, the important thing is that you have arrived, and now the party can really begin!"

Preoccupation with your present circumstances can be costly. We have millions of divorces each year, and many of them are related to the inability or unwillingness of one or both of the partners to listen. And we have witnessed needless tragedies—where lives were lost: the *Titanic*, Pearl Harbor, the *Challenger*, Katrina, COVID-19—because someone was too preoccupied to listen to the information being given to them. Equally as destructive is preoccupation with your past experiences.

To counteract your preoccupations, remind yourself, throughout the conversation or throughout the meeting, to "Focus. Focus. Focus."

Don't Be Misled by Your Past Experience

If, for example, your weekly staff meetings have almost always been a waste of time, you may enter a meeting expecting to learn nothing. You may use your past experience to prejudge the communication that is about to take place, prejudging it as either unworthy of your time or nothing more than what you've heard before. Of course, you could be right, but you might also *miss* some important things you need to know.

Or you may *misinterpret* the meaning of something—if you only rely on your past experience, and if you fail to ask the right questions. Kids do this all the time. One of my audience members, an in-home nursing director, talked about taking her four-year-old daughter with her as she visited her elderly shut-in patients. She said her daughter was especially intrigued with all the canes, walkers, wheelchairs, and other equipment used by the patients. But one day she found her daughter staring at a pair of false teeth soaking in a glass. As she braced herself for a barrage of questions, her daughter merely turned and whispered, "The tooth fairy will never believe this!"

If you catch yourself prejudging what someone is going to say, if you're not sure what you might have missed in the other person's comments, just say, "Excuse me. Would you please go over that last point again?"

When you *decide* to listen, when you *assume* responsibility for understanding, you've taken another giant step toward compassionate listening.

Listening Skill #3: Position Yourself to Listen

If you're about to have a one-on-one conversation with someone or gather together for a staff meeting, whether in person or via a video chat that includes folks from numerous countries, put yourself in a *position* to do nothing but listen. It will make all the difference in the world when it comes to your attention, comprehension, retention, and may even affect how much people like and trust you. Here are some ways to help you position yourself:

- **Remove or reduce physical barriers.**
  When there are things between you and the other person, listening can become more difficult. If you're on a job site, for example, and there's a piece of equipment between you and the other person, it will be harder to hear as well as pay attention. If there's a desk between you and somebody else, the desk may imply that one person is above the other, and that kind of discomfort will disrupt the listening process. For example, one researcher found that only 11 percent of patients are at ease when the doctor sits behind a desk, but 55 percent of the patients are at ease when the desk is removed.
- **Minimize distractions.**
  Put aside everything and anything that is not related to the listening process you're supposed to be engaged in. Don't try to read your text messages at the same time you're listening to your colleague. Don't try to watch the television at the same time your spouse is talking to you. These actions suggest you have more important things to do than listen to the other person. It will undoubtedly lower your listening effectiveness and damage your relationships—especially if you get caught.

  Whenever possible and practical, don't allow yourself to be interrupted. While you're talking to someone, don't answer the phone, open the door, sign some documents, or try to do something else at the same time. The same goes for virtual or video conference meetings. You can't expect to multi-task without a noticeable drop in understanding. Just focus on each other and what is being said.
- **Lean forward and face the person you are talking to.**
  When you do this, your nonverbal communication is saying, "I want to hear what you have to say. I don't want to miss a single word. Please go ahead." You're demonstrating your

commitment to the communication process, and you encourage the speaker to share fully, openly, and honestly. However, if you lean back in your chair or get too relaxed, your attention will wander. Effective listening is active rather than passive, laid back, and taking it easy.

- **Use lots of eye contact.**

    Look at the other person when he or she is speaking to you, or look at each individual in your meeting as he or she speaks. Don't fool yourself into thinking you can "sorta" listen and at the same time sneak in a few glances at your incoming e-mail, your watch, and your desk filled with work—and get away with it. You can't! No matter how good you are or think you are at multitasking, if you do anything other than look at and listen to the person who is speaking, you're communicating disrespect. The other person will always wonder if you care more about those things than you do about him and what he has to say. And that would be the exact opposite of compassionate listening.

Listening Skill #4: Listen with an Open Mind

The communication and listening processes are strange phenomena. A message can travel around the world in a matter of seconds. But it can take years to travel that last inch into your brain if you have preconceived ideas standing in your way.

Manage Your Tune-Out Buttons

You're a normal human being. You have feelings. But as a champion, you cannot let your feelings get in the way of your listening.

For example, some words are so emotionally charged that as soon as you hear them, you shut down. Your tune-out button is up and working, and you stop listening. It could be the B word, the N word, and the F word that you find so utterly offensive. It could be sexist phrases used by a coworker, like "baby," "honey," "sweetie pie," or "beefcake." Or it could be cursing comments made by a spouse or a customer, all of which you find disrespectful and unprofessional.

Of course, using language like that is usually considered inappropriate and morally reprehensible. And you may have a host of other words, phrases, and topics that are so emotional for you that once they're brought up, it's difficult for you to keep on talking with any degree of rationality or keep on listening with any degree of true understanding. These are tune-out buttons for you.

Just because you don't approve of the way someone says something does not mean you should stop listening to what he or she has to say. Sometimes you need to know what that person is saying. And yes, there may be a need and a time to confront people on their use of language, but you must understand their message—first. Don't go into emotional overdrive right then and there.

To manage your tune-out buttons, remind yourself to stay calm and in control. Remind yourself to *thoughtfully respond* to what is being said rather than *emotionally react* to what is being said. Don't let the other person's inappropriate remark or your own hypersensitivity destroy your listening effectiveness.

Keep Your Confirmation Bias in Check

This is difficult because we all have confirmation bias. In other words, you tend to believe certain things and then tune into only those bits of information that confirm what you already believe. In fact it's one of the biggest obstacles to *the process of compassionate listening*.

For example, you may be guilty of entering conversations with preconceived ideas about another person or his topic of discussion. And once you have a preconceived idea in mind, it's almost impossible to "hear" what the other person is saying. Your preconceptions act as a filter and you only hear what supports your preconceptions.

I see confirmation bias everywhere. I see it when managers ask, "What can you expect from the staff?" Their preconceived notions get in the way of any open-minded listening to their staff.

I see it when the employees say, "You can't trust what they're saying at the top." More preconceived notions blocking any open-minded listening to their leaders.

I see it when customer service providers talk about their difficult customers, saying, "They're all alike." Still more evidence of confirmation bias rather than effective listening.

And now with our country in disarray, we've moved from a somewhat natural, troubling confirmation bias to an overheated, emotionally rabid confirmation bias. So much so that most people only listen to the news outlets that support their preconceived political bias. Without even thinking about it, let alone seek out and listen to all the information, they automatically label the news from their pre-selected outlets as the truth and news from other sources as lies.

That's dangerous. When you don't listen to the whole truth, you endanger your work teams, your marriage, and even your nation. You're bound to make some bad decisions. But when you keep your confirmation bias in check, when you listen to and hear *all* the information being presented, you become a much better listener, not to mention a better person. That's why the *Bible* says in John 8:32 (NIV), "The truth will set you free."

Take a moment to acknowledge your own confirmation biases so they don't unconsciously trip you up. Be aware of the people, topics, positions, points of view, and news sources where you instantly accept or reject whatever they have to say. Once you're aware of those biases you can control them.

The same thing applies to your stereotypes. To keep them in check and stop them from killing off your listening effectiveness, become aware of the kinds of people that turn you off. When you're listening to them, remind yourself that you don't have to like them or even agree with everything they say. All you have to do is give their comments a fair hearing to see if you can learn anything you can use.

Beware of Charisma

The charisma of the message sender may affect how well you listen. You see this in politics all the time. Quite often, candidates are chosen and elected not so much for the brilliance of their thought as the brilliance of their delivery. A charismatic politician can make a tired, trivial, stupid, or just-plain-wrong message seem new, exciting, and right, fooling the listener into thinking that he or she doesn't even have to question or clarify the message.

Perhaps this has happened to you. You got so carried away by someone's charisma that you stopped listening to anyone else or any other message that did not agree with your charismatic speaker. You traded your open mind for a closed mind, shutting down your listening effectiveness and intellectual acuity in the process. Or you may have failed to listen to someone who had something important to say simply because that speaker's delivery was dull. If so, remind yourself that *what* a person says is 10 times more important than *how* he or she says it.

Listening Skill #5: Ask More Questions

As my colleague Michael Atlshuler says, "What people say is unimportant; what people *mean* by what they say is everything." And the only way you're going to know what they mean is through the art of asking questions. Here are a few ideas about how to do that.

Get More Information

When you ask for more information, it replaces assumptions with realities. One of the easiest ways to do this is to use the word "and" with a pause and questioning tone to your voice. Perhaps a colleague is telling you about an incident at work. You listen carefully to his story, but want to learn more. Just ask, "And?" Pause for a moment and the other person will invariably go on and give you more information.

Or you could use the three magical words of "Help me understand" or "Tell me more." When used with a nonthreatening, inquisitive tone of voice and appropriate facial expressions, you encourage the other person to give you more details. You come across as someone who really cares about the other person rather than someone who is grilling the speaker.

Encourage More Depth

Ask open-ended questions that start with the five W's and the one H: who, what, when, where, why, and how. Unlike questions that can be answered with a simple "yes" or "no," open-ended questions encourage a speaker to go beyond the superficial and go deeper. If you ask brave questions that you typically do not discuss, you build the foundation for a stronger relationship, just like I did with my grandmother.

When you listen to someone's response to these questions, do more than listen *to* that someone; listen *for* something. If the other person is describing a situation, *listen for the facts*, the key points, or the main ideas she is giving. Behind every fact there is a feeling. *Listen for those feelings*, whether or not they are expressed. You'll get a lot more out of the conversation. You will also stay much more alert and engaged in the conversation than you would if you just sat back, did nothing, and merely waited for the other person to finish talking.

Clarify the Facts

As Alan Greenspan, the former chairman of the Federal Reserve Bank put it, "I know you think you understand what you thought I said, but I'm not sure you realize that what you heard is not what I meant."[3]

You've got to clarify the facts. And the only way you can do that is to rephrase what you heard the other person say and ask him or her if that is correct. Instead of assuming you understand the other person, use such phrases as, "If I'm hearing you correctly, you're saying . . ." And ask things like, "Do you mean . . ." It's not enough to just nod your head, grunt "uh-huh," and wait for the next silent spot so you can say what you want to say.

When you get into the habit of asking questions to clarify the facts, two very positive things take place in the process of compassionate listening. First, you tend to stay with the speaker instead of planning your next remark. Second, you're telling others that they and their message are so important that you want to make sure you got it right. And whether you initially understand or misunderstand the message the other person shares, you both win. If you get the speaker's message right, he'll feel good and affirm you. If you get the message wrong, he'll clarify.

Define the Slippery Words Being Used

Almost any word can be interpreted in more than one way. That can easily cause communication breakups. But untrained listeners don't even think about that. They hear something and automatically think they've got it. More often than not, they don't.

Some words are much more likely to cause listening difficulties than others, and you have to be especially diligent when you hear someone use them. Sales trainer Jeff Thull calls them "fat words."[4] Words such as *almost, maybe, might, quality, soon, user friendly, easy,* and *improved* are fatter or much more slippery than others. There are dozens if not hundreds of different things each of those words could mean.

For example, if you are a salesperson and your prospect tells you, "I'm not sure your level of quality will meet our requirements," what would be your most likely response? To give a sales pitch about your product or service? It would be the exact wrong thing to do. As Thull states, "It's not appropriate to answer a statement as if it were a question"[5] because you don't even know what your prospect is saying.

The prospect's statement is filled with slippery words. You have no idea what he means by "not sure," "level of quality," and "meet our requirements." To eliminate this listening challenge, you have to clarify or define the slippery words before you respond to them. Ask such things as, "You mentioned 'level of quality.' To make sure I really understand that, can you please tell me your quality requirements?"

Clarify Feelings

Whenever you're communicating with another person, you can be sure of one thing. The other person always has some feelings going on, whether it's about the current situation, your present topic of conversation, or a hundred other things. The other person may or may not be aware of those feelings, and may or may not be expressing those feelings, but the feelings are there nonetheless. And sometimes it's critically important to understand those feelings before a problem can be resolved or the relationship improved.

If that seems to be the case, use a perception-check question. You could say something like, "You seem rather concerned about that new product line," or "You sound somewhat disappointed by my remark. Is that right?" You're not judging the other person's feelings or telling the other person how to feel. You're simply extending the courtesy of telling the other person what you're picking up and giving that person the chance to set you straight about what she is feeling. It's polite, respectful, and most often relationship building.

Listening Skill #6: Refrain from Interrupting

This is a very difficult skill for some people to master. They're used to hearing someone say a few words and then jumping in with their own comments. In fact, they're so used to saying things like "that reminds me of . . ." "let me tell you about . . ." or "that's nothing compared to what I went through," that it almost seems natural and right.

Well, it may seem natural, but it's not right. When you interrupt someone, it's a sure sign that you're not using the *process of compassionate listening*, and you don't care that much about the other person's comments. And that's not a good place for any relationship to be.

Interruptions seem to be especially tempting when someone comes to you with a problem. You may want to jump right in and give advice. More often than not, however, the other person simply wants you to listen patiently.

Of course, this sounds good in theory, right? But what if you're pressed for time? You may be thinking if you don't interrupt the other person, if you don't stop the other person from talking, you'll be late for something else. That may be true. In that case, tell the other person that you'd like to give him or her your full attention, but that's not possible at the moment. Agree on a time the two of you can continue the conversation when you may give it your very best attention.

We're all busy these days. So it's very tempting to try to speed things up in a conversation by interrupting the other person. But that's usually a poor trade-off. Typically, it takes a lot less time to get the information right the first time than to straighten out all the misunderstandings later on.

Listening Skill #7: Slow Down Your Back-and-Forth Exchange

Too many people are guilty of jumping into a conversation with their response the very moment the other person stops talking. Some people even jump in before the other person stops talking. (We just talked about interrupting.) The problem is it seldom works. It almost always hurts the listening process and the people involved in the discussion. But this is what does work.

- **Adopt the Acknowledgment Technique.**
  Specifically, when someone is talking to you, instead of jumping in with your response as soon as the other person finishes, you must first acknowledge the fact that you heard what she had to say. It could be as simple as saying, "Interesting point . . ." "I know what you mean . . ." or "If I understand you correctly . . ." Comment on what the other person said before you give your response. It will force you to spend more time listening to what is being said than thinking about what you're going to say next.
- **Try the Three-Gulp Rule.**
  Bob Parsons, executive coach at Parsons Coaching and Consulting, taught me this. When Bob hears someone share an important point, he does not give an immediate response, outside of a nonverbal acknowledgment such as a nod of the head or a verbal "hmm." He then ponders what he heard and how he's going to respond as he takes three gulps of water. It gives him time to think about his response, and it tells the other person he's going to get a thoughtful response rather than a flippant, off-the-cuff remark.

Both techniques work works wonders. They offer respect to both parties in the conversation. And they eliminate the fast and furious give-and-take communication that characterizes most of the political talk shows these days—and many business meetings and marital conflicts as well.

Listening Skill #8: Reinforce Your Retention

Of all the listening skills I've addressed thus far, this is the one I need the most. I'm all too guilty of hearing someone tell me something and then forgetting what they told me. Just ask my wife or kids. Perhaps you're in the same boat with me. So what can we do about it? I've found two things that work:

- **Listen for value.**
  When someone else is talking, ask yourself such questions as: "Why do I need to know this? How can I use this information? And how will this information help me, my life, my work, or my relationships?" The more value you consciously attach to someone's comment, the longer you will remember it.

- **Use mental reviews.**
  When you're listening to someone, periodically review what the other person is saying and has said. In a few seconds, you can mentally review everything a presenter has said in the past hour at a work seminar, or you can review everything your spouse was sharing about the challenges of her day. This little technique not only doubles your listening retention, but it also keeps your mind from wandering to other thoughts.

The Payoff in Compassionate Listening

When people say they love their significant other but never listens to them, I know they're either lying or don't know how to listen. When managers say they care about their teammates, but those same teammates say the boss never listens to them, I know that manager may have good intentions, but not good listening skills. If you really care about the people in your life, you will care about listening to them, and you will use the eight skills of compassionate listening.

If you do, you're going to get some significant payoffs. Indeed, I've noticed that when I use these skills my business improves, my relationships are strengthened, and my life goes better. I even get smarter. As American columnist Doug Larson writes, "Wisdom is the reward you get for a lifetime of listening when you would have preferred to talk."[6] The same will be true for you.

PART IV

Passage

CHAPTER 14

The Champion Edge Works

It's Time to End the Craziness and Sadness

Imagine a plane full of passengers. The captain comes on the intercom and says, "Thank you for choosing our airline. I'm not exactly sure when we'll take off or when we'll arrive. As a matter of fact, I'm not even sure where we're going or how we're going to get there. Hopefully, our fuel tank has enough gas, and we'll get to where you want to go at the right time. For now, just sit back and enjoy the ride."

You would probably think, "That's the scariest thing I've ever heard." Yet, that's the way a lot of people live. They have no particular direction for their life or their career, and they lack the energy and skill to accomplish their goals. They're just putting in time and hoping it all works out.

That's crazy. That's settling for a lot less than you could accomplish if you only had *The Champion Edge* working for you.

It's also sad. You could have good intentions, work your butt off, and never come close to turning your life and career dreams into reality. All because you have mistakenly bought into some flavor-of-the-month business fad or pop psychology filled with clever catchphrases that don't deliver what they promise.

For example, some people will say they follow the old adage, "If it is to be, it's up to me." On the surface it sounds good. There's only one problem with the phrase: it leaves you hanging in midair. It doesn't tell you *where* you're going because it lacks *purpose*. It doesn't tell *what's* going to take you there because it lacks *passion*. And it doesn't tell *how* you're going to get there because it lacks *process*.

That's the problem with so many positive-thinking books, self-help routines, and career manuals. They don't give you *the whole formula for success*. Which brings us back to the very beginning of this book and the two questions that have bugged me all my life.

First, why do some people accomplish so much more than others in their business careers and lives? And second, why do some people accomplish so much more than others—so much more quickly?

You now have the answer to those two questions. The highest achieving people, personally and professionally, have *The Champion Edge* working for them. And so can you.

Integrate and Activate

Above I just mentioned the phrase, *the whole formula for success*. That's what *The Champion Edge* is all about. From my experience and research, it can be summarized in a simple formula: Purpose + Passion + Process = Passage.

However, to get champion results, you must *integrate* all three elements into every aspect of your life and work all at the same time. You can't focus on being *purpose*-driven in your career and forget about your *purpose* in life and expect to be happy. You can't have a pumped-up *passion*-ate attitude at home but have a lackluster attitude at work and expect to achieve much. And you can't use the proper communication *process* with your customers but fail to use the same *process* with your loved ones and expect to have profitable results. *The Champion Edge* is about a new way of thinking and behaving so you're always purpose-driven, passion-filled, and process-guided, on and off the job.

You must also *activate* all three elements of the formula before you can expect to get the full *passage* to the success you want. And most people overlook one or more of these key elements. Some people work hard, but without a clearly defined *purpose*, nothing is very fulfilling. Other people have great dreams, but without an enduring *passion*, they give up before they see the *passage*. And still other people have the best of intentions and positive attitudes, but they lack the *process* for turning it into reality.

In other words, you've got to activate *The Champion Edge* now. Don't fall into the "as-soon-as" trap that says "as soon as I get the time and energy . . ." or "as soon as certain things happen . . ." or "as soon as I get around to it, I'll give *The Champion Edge* a try."

Author, track star, and cardiologist Dr. George Sheehan talked about those soon-as, non-champion kinds of people who are forever waiting. He said, "There are those of us who are always about to live. We are waiting until things change, until there is more time, until we are less tired, until we get a promotion, until we settle down—until, until, until. It always seems as if there is some major event that must occur in our lives before we begin living."[1] Don't be like those kinds of people. *Activate* now!

A Tried-and-True Formula

I said it above, but it is worth repeating. *The Champion Edge* can be summarized in a simple formula: Purpose + Passion + Process = Passage.

Amazingly enough, the formula brings the spiritual, psychological, and business worlds together. Virtually every spiritual belief or major religion emphasizes the critical importance of finding your *purpose* and living on purpose. The psychological research is filled with studies that document the power of *passion* or having the characteristics of attitude, persistence, and character working for you. And the business world continually focuses on the *process* that brings the best results.

I find it extremely satisfying, to know that this formula is supported by years and years of belief, research, and everyday experience. And I find it extremely motivating that there isn't a part of your life or career that cannot be enhanced by this formula.

I've experienced it firsthand. The evidence can be seen in everything from my health and finances to my goals and relationships. The evidence can be seen in my business growth, from a kid walking the streets selling door-to-door to being inducted into the Speaker Hall of Fame.

I've seen the new-and-complete you take place in the lives and careers of hundreds of thousands of people. You've read a few of their stories in this book.

I'll never forget the first time I consciously noticed how this formula could and did change lives. I was in high school when Richard Chaput spoke at our high school assembly. He was rolled onto the stage, flat on his back, encased in an iron lung. Even though there were several hundred students in the auditorium, you could have heard a pin drop when he uttered his opening line: "Every dream I've ever had I've been able to accomplish."

He began to share his story. When Richard was nine years old, he was diagnosed with polio. The disease left him completely paralyzed. His paralysis was so severe he had to breathe by physically gulping for air, somewhat like a frog. At night, he slept in an iron lung.

Initially, Richard did not handle it well. He gave into self-pity, until one day his parish priest helped him snap out of it by letting him know his life wasn't over. There was a *reason* he was alive and with the right *attitude* and *plan*, he had a life of achievement and satisfaction ahead of him. (It sounds a bit like *The Champion Edge*, doesn't it?) From that moment on, Richard started living with *purpose* and *passion*, and he put a *process* in place where he would help others by speaking to any group that would listen to his story—including audiences at the White House with two different U.S. presidents.

As a teenager sitting in his audience, I was stunned as Richard talked about writing books and speaking to thousands. I was inspired by what a person could accomplish with a driving sense of *purpose*, a healthy dose of *passion*, and a practical set of *processes*. That's why I'll never forget his closing line: "Life is a banquet, but most people are starving to death" because, as he implied, they don't have these three elements working for them.

If Richard Chaput could experience *The Champion Edge*, then there's no reason you can't too.

Notes

Chapter 1

1. (Emmett 2009)
2. (Noble n.d.)
3. (Hilton n.d.)
4. (Schwartz n.d.)
5. (Sheehan and Sheehan 2013)
6. (Maltz 1960)
7. (Washington 1901)
8. (Geneen n.d.)

Chapter 2

1. (Beck 2012)
2. (Dr. Purushothaman 2014)
3. (Hemingway and Hotchner 2008)
4. ("Study Shows Achievers Share Certain Traits." 1982)
5. (Purushothaman n.d.)
6. (Saunders 2007)

Chapter 3

1. (McGuire and Abitz 2001)
2. (Forbes.com. 2016)
3. (Ellsworth 2002)
4. (Roth 2011)
5. (Buettner 2008)
6. (Nietzsche 2009)
7. (Kornblum 2014)

Chapter 4

1. (Parachin 2001)
2. (Georgy 2008)
3. (Porras, Emery, and Thompson 2007)
4. (Leider 2010)
5. (Buford 2008)

Chapter 5

1. (Tracy n.d.)
2. (Miller n.d.)
3. (Andy 2009)
4. (Skip Downing 2011)
5 (Oppong n.d.)

Chapter 6

1. "Mahoney's Career Switch Pays Off." 1994.
2. (Pritchett 1999)
3. Proverbs 26:20 (The Living Bible)
4. (Woodbury n.d.)
5. This quote is most often attributed to Coolidge. It was printed in a pamphlet in the 1930s by New York Life Insurance, Co. where Coolidge served as a director.

Chapter 7

1. (DeFord 2004)
2. (Gordon 2012)
3. "Quotes by Earl Nightingale about Attitude." n.d.
4. (Jarrow 2013)
5. (James 2002)
6. (Webb 2002)
7. Philippians 4:8 (The Living Bible)
8. (Zuck 2009)
9. (Anderson 1995)

10. (Reinhold 2001)
11. (Ward 1970)

Chapter 8

1. (Eshun 2013)
2. (Mackay n.d.)
3. (Savage 1985)
4. (Demakis 2012)
5. (Calhoun 2013)
6. (Kimbro 2011)
7. (Riverol 1992)
8. (Buckley 2004)
9. (Pettitt and Wolff 1966)
10. (Franklin 1996)
11. ("Lucy Goes to the Hospital." March 18, 2014)
12. ("I Love Lucy." 2014)
13. Lee and Little 1997

Chapter 9

1. (Woolman 2007)
2. (Shilling 2014)
3. (Jones 2012)
4. (Zuck 2009)
5. (Boone and Kurtz 2014)
6. (Aiken and Keller 2007)
7. (Sharp 2002)
8. (Nietzsche 2002)
9. (Heffernan n.d.)
10. (Hyatt 2012)
11. (Gayeski 2004)
12. (Crouch 2003)
13. (Josephson 2012)
14. (Ortberg 2007)
15. (Dill 2006)

Chapter 11

1. (Baker 2013)
2. (Williamson 1986)
3. (Allen 2003)
4. (Whitmore 2005)
5. (Morgan 2009)
6. (Anderson 2013)
7. (Palahniuk 2005)
8. (Lemonick and Mankato 2001)

Chapter 12

1. (Kinlaw 1995)
2. (Chapman 2009)
3. (Levin 2009)
4. (Giblin 2010)
5. (Levin 2009)
6. (Brinkman 2013)
7. (David and Claudia Arp 2010)
8. (Blanchard 2010)
9. (Boggan and VerSteeg 1997)

Chapter 13

1. (Husman, Lahiff, and Penrose 1988)
2. (Haney 1979)
3. ("Alan Greenspan Quotes." n.d.)
4. (Thull 2010)
5. Ibid.
6. (Weis 2010)

Chapter 14

1. (Sheehan and Sheehan 2013)

References

1982. "Study Shows Achievers Share Certain Traits." *The Telegraph*, 37.

1994. "Mahoney's Career Switch Pays Off." *New Straits Times*, 23. February 10

2014. "I Love Lucy." *Wikipedia*, last modified July 28, 2014, http://en.wikipedia. org/wiki/I_Love_Lucy

Aiken, C.B., and S.P. Keller. February 2007. "The CEO's Role in Leading Transformation." *Insights and Publications*, http://mckinsey.com/insights/ organization/the_ceos_role_in_leading_transformation

Allen, J.D. 2003. *Humans in Training: Everything You Need, You Already Have*, 133. Orange County, CA: HIT Pub.

Anderson, D. 1995. *Act Now!: Successful Acting Techniques You Can Use Everyday to Dramatically Improve Health, Wealth and Relationships*. New York, NY: John Wiley & Sons.

Anderson, J. 2013. *Principle-Based Leadership: Driving Your Success as a Leader*, 167. Bloomington, IN: iUniverse.

Andy. 2009. "Time Management Techniques: Tomorrows Top 6." on the *Time Management Blog*, http://time-management-techniques.com/ time-management-techniques-tomorrows-top-6.html

Baker, J. 2013. *Life's Healing Choices*, 129. New York, NY: Howard Books.

Beck, F. 2012. *Cultivating the Fine Art of Selfishness: Improving Community by Empowering Individuals*, 9. Charleston, SC: Advantage Media Group.

Blanchard, K. 2010. "Praise v. Criticism." *How We Lead Blog*, July 13, 2010, http://howwelead.org/2010/07/13/praise-v-criticism/

Boggan, D., and A. VerSteeg. 1997. *Confessions of an UnManager*, 64. Durham, NC: Dartnell.

Boone, L., and D. Kurtz. 2014. *Contemporary Marketing, Update 2015*, 84. Boston: Cengage Learning.

Brinkman, S. 2013. "Survey: Families Spend Less Than 8 Hours Together Per Week." *The Women of Grace Blog*, July 16, 2013, http://womenofgrace.com/ blog/?p=22778

Buckley, J. 2004. *Muhammad Ali*, 1970. New York, NY: Gareth Stevens.

Buettner, D. November/December 2008. "Find Purpose, Live Longer." *AARP Magazine*.

Buford, B. 2008. *Halftime*, 121. Grand Rapids, MI: Zondervan.

Calhoun, R. 2013. *Life in the Image of God*, 28. Bloomington, IN: Westbow Press.

Chapman, G.D. 2009. *The Marriage You've Always Wanted*. Chicago, IL: Moody.

Crouch, T. 2003. *Truth or Dare: Do You Have the Courage to Change Your Life?*, 191. Springville, UT: Cedar Fort.

David and Claudia Arp. 2010. *The Second Half of Marriage*. Grand Rapids, MI: Zondervan.

DeFord, D. 2004. *1000 Brilliant Achievement Quotes*, 12. Omaha: Ordinary People Can Win!.

Demakis, J. 2012. *The Ultimate Book of Quotations*, 205. Raleigh, NC: Lulu.

Dill, J.G. 2006. *Myth, Fact, and Navigators' Secrets: Incredible Tales of the Sea and Sailors*, 51. Guilford, CT: Globe Pequot.

Dr. Purushothaman, ed. 2014. *Words of Wisdom (Volume 25): 1001 Quotes and Quotations*, 144. Kollam, Kerala, India: Centre for Human Perfection.

Ellsworth, R.R. 2002. *Leading with Purpose: The New Corporate Realities*, 94. Stanford: Stanford University Press.

Emmett, R. 2009. *Manage Your Time to Reduce Your Stress: A Handbook for the Overworked, Overscheduled, and Overwhelmed*, 110. New York, NY: Bloomsbury.

Eshun, B.A. 2013. *How to Start Your Business with or without Money: A Practical Approach to 'Small Beginnings'*, 114. Victoria, BC: Trafford.

Forbes.com. November 13, 2016. "3 Reasons Why The Power of Purpose is Unquestionable." https://forbes.com/sites/jeffboss/2016/11/13/3-reasons-why-the-power-of-purpose-is-unquestionable/#792fcce1764f

Franklin, B. 1996. *The Autobiography of Benjamin Franklin*, 123. Mineola, NY: Dover.

Gayeski, D.M. 2004. *Managing Learning and Communication Systems as Business Assets*, 8. New York, NY: Pearson/Prentice Hall.

Geneen, H.S. n.d. https://inspirationalstories.com/quotes/t/harold-s-geneen/

Georgy. 2008. "How Temple Baptist Church, Philadelphia, Came into Being." on the *Turn Back to God Blog*, September 15, 2008, http://turnbacktogod. com/ story-how-temple-baptist-church-philadelphia-came-into-being/

Giblin, L. 2010. *Skill with People*, 13. rev. ed.

Gordon, J. 2012. *The Positive Dog: A Story About the Power of Positivity*, 6. New York, NY: John Wiley & Sons.

Haney, W.V. 1979. *Communication and Interpersonal Relations*. Homestead, IL: Irwin.

Heffernan, M.A. n.d. *The Naked Truth: A Working Woman's Manifesto on Business and What Really Matters*, 84. New York, NY: John Wiley & Sons.

Hemingway, E., and A.E. Hotchner. 2008. *The Good Life According to Hemingway*, 30. New York, NY: HarperCollins.

Hilton, C. n.d. http://finestquotes.com/author_quotes-author-Conrad+Hilton-page-0.htm

Husman, R.C., J.M. Lahiff, and J.M. Penrose. 1988. *Business Communication: Strategies and Skills*. Chicago: Dryden Press.

Hyatt, M. 2012. *Platform: Get Noticed in a Noisy World*. Nashville, TN: Thomas Nelson.

Ibid.

James, W. 2002. https://goodreads.com/quotes/10301-the-greatest-discovery-of-any-generation-is-that-a-human

Jarrow, C. 2013. "7 Ways a Positive Attitude Can Make You More Productive." *Time Management Ninja*, November 18, 2013, http://timemanagementninja.com.

Jones, C.D. 2012. *Inspirational Being*, 65. Raleigh, NC: Lulu.

Josephson, M. 2012. "Commentaries, the Nature of Character." *What Will Matter*, October 22, 2012, http://whatwillmatter.com/2012/10/commentary-798-2-the-nature-of-character/

Kimbro, D. 2011. *Daily Motivations for African-American Success*, 57. New York, NY: Random House.

Kinlaw, D.C. 1995. *The Practice of Empowerment*, 60. Brookfield, VT: Gower.

Kornblum, J. 2014. "For Kirk Douglas and Wife, the Playground's the Thing." *USA Today*, May 26, 2008, http://usatoday30.usatoday. com/life/people/2008-05-26-kirk-douglas-playgrounds_N.htm (accessed July 28, 2014).

Lee, B., and J. Little. 1997. *Jeet Kune Do: Bruce Lee's Commentaries on the Martial Way*, 363. North Clarendon, VT: Tuttle.

Leider, R. 2010. *The Power of Purpose*, 22. San Francisco: Berrett-Koehler Publishers.

Lemonick, M.D., and A.P. Mankato. 2001. "Nun Study: How One Scientist and 678 Sisters Are Helping Unlock the Secrets of Alzhiemer's." *Time*, May 14, 2001, http://content.time.com/time/world/article/0,8599,2047984,00.html

Levin, D.L. 2009. *Don't Just Talk, Be Heard!*. Minneapolis, MN: Minneapolis Press.

Mackay, H. n.d. "Success Is a Marathon." http://inc.com/harvey-mackay/success-is-a-marathon.html (accessed April 3, 2012).

Maltz, M. 1960. *Psycho-Cybernetics*. New York, NY: Simon & Schuster.

McGuire, C., and D. Abitz. 2001. *The Best Advice Ever for Teachers*, 145. Kansas City, MO: Andrews McMeel Publishing.

Miller, S. n.d. *Oomph Power! How to Get Re-Energized for Outrageous Success*, 51.. Avinger, TX: Simpson-Wesley.

Morgan, T. 2009. *Killing Cockroaches*, 57. Nashville: B&H.

n.d. "Alan Greenspan Quotes." *Goodreads*, http://goodreads.com/quotes/204034-i-know-you-think-you-understand-what-you-thought

n.d. "Lucy Goes to the Hospital." *Wikipedia*, last modified March 18, 2014, http://en.wikipedia.org/wiki/Lucy_Goes_to_the_Hospital

n.d. "Quotes by Earl Nightingale about Attitude." *Online Quotations Book*, http://quotationsbook.com/quote/3493/

Nietzsche, F. 2002. *Nietzsche: Beyond Good & Evil: Prelude to a Philosophy of the Future*, 74. Trans. Walter Kaufmann. New York, NY: Cambridge University Press.

Nietzsche, F. 2009. *Götzen-Dämmerung, oder, Wie man mit dem Hammer Notes 257 philosophiert* [Twilight of the Idols, or, How to Philosophize with a Hammer], 12. Oxford University Press.

Noble, C.C. n.d. https://institutesuccess.com/library/you-must-have-long-term-goals-to-keep-you-from-being-frustrated-by-short-term-failures-charles-c-noble-2/

Oppong, T. n.d. "Why Everyone Needs a Life Philosophy." https://thriveglobal.com/stories/spell-out-life-philosophy/

Ortberg, J. 2007. *When the Game Is Over, It All Goes Back in the Box*. Grand Rapids, MI: Zondervan.

Palahniuk, C. 2005. *Fight Club: A Novel*, 46. New York, NY: W.W. Norton.

Parachin, V.M. March–April 2001. *Being a Father Who Makes a Difference*, 12. Scouting.

Pettitt, R.E.L., and B. Wolff. 1966. *The Drive Within Me*, 10. New York, NY: Prentice Hall.

Philippians 4:8 (The Living Bible).

Porras, J.I., S. Emery, and M. Thompson. 2007. *Success Built to Last*, 25. Upper Saddle River, NJ: Wharton School Publishing.

Pritchett, P. 1999. *The Employee Handbook of New Work Habits for the Next Millennium*10. Dallas: Pritchett Rummler-Brache.

Proverbs 26:20 (The Living Bible).

Purushothaman, ed. n.d. *Words of Wisdom*, 144.

Reinhold, B.B. 2001. *Free to Succeed: Designing the Life You Want in the New Free Agent Economy*, 131. New York: Plume.

Riverol, A. 1992. *Live from Atlantic City: The History of the Miss America Pageant*, 132. Bowling Green, OH: Bowling Green State University Popular Press.

Roth, B. 2011. *Be More Productive—Slow Down: Design the Life and Work You Want*, 70. Bloomington, IN: iUniverse.

Saunders, D. 2007. *Big Eyes*, 10. Charleston, SC: Advantage Media Group.

Savage, D.G. 1985. "Interviews with 120 Top Artists, Athletes, and Scholars: The Key to Success? It's Drive, Not Talent, Study Finds." *Los Angeles Times*, February 17, 1985, http://articles.latimes.com/1985-02-17/news/mn-3575_1_top-artists

Schwartz, D.C. n.d. https://pinterest.com/pin/485051822363076950/

Sharp, M.J. 2002 "The Top Ten Ways to Change a Mediocre Employee into a High Performing One." *Articles Factory*, October 6, 2002, http://articlesfactory.com/articles/business/the-top-ten-ways-to-change-a-mediocre-employee-into-a-high-performing-one.html

Sheehan, G., and A. Sheehan. 2013. *The Essential Sheehan: A Lifetime of Running Wisdom from the Legendary Dr. George Sheehan*, 14. Emmaus, PA: Rodale.

Sheehan, G., and A. Sheehan. 2013. *The Essential Sheehan: A Lifetime of Running Wisdom from the Legendary Dr. George Sheehan*, 44. Emmaus, PA: Rodale.

Shilling, D.A. 2014. *It's Showtime in Rochester*, 47. Victor, NY: Pancoast.

Skip Downing. 2011. *On Course*, 105. Boston: Cengage Learning.

This quote is most often attributed to Coolidge. It was printed in a pamphlet in the 1930s by New York Life Insurance, Co. where Coolidge served as a director.

Thull, J. 2010. *Mastering the Complex Sale: How to Compete and Win When the Stakes Are High!*, 153. New York, NY: John Wiley & Sons.

Tracy, B. "Success Through Goal Setting, Part 1 Of 3." https://briantracy.com/blog/personal-success/success-through-goal-setting-part-1-of-3/

Ward, W.A. 1970. *Fountains of Faith*. Anderson, SC: Droke House.

Washington, B.T. 1901. *Up from Slavery: An Autobiography, Booker T. Washington*. Doubleday & Co.

Webb, V. 2002. *Florence Nightingale: The Making of a Radical Theologian*, 80. Atlanta: Chalice Press.

Weis, D. 2010. *Everlasting Wisdom*, 69. Trowbridge, Wiltshire, England: Paragon.

Whitmore, J. 2005. *Business Class: Etiquette Essentials for Success at Work*, 48. New York, NY: Macmillan.

Williamson, J.N. 1986. *The Leader Manager*, 87. New York, NY: John Wiley & Sons.

Woodbury, D. n.d. "Casual Friday Elizabeth Edwards Quote on Having a Positive Attitude." on *Where We Go Now Blog*, http://wherewegonow.com/category/tags/elizabeth-edwards

Woolman, J. 2007. *The Journal of John Woolman*, 201. Rockville, MD: Wildside Press.

Zuck, R.B. 2009. *The Speaker's Quote Book: Over 5,000 Illustrations and Quotations for All Occasions*, 243. Grand Rapids: Kregel Academic and Professional.

Zuck, R.B. 2009. *The Speaker's Quote Book: Over 5,000 Illustrations and Quotations for All Occasions*, 58. Grand Rapids: Kregel Academic.

About the Author

At the age of 7, **Alan R. Zimmerman** was selling greeting cards door-to-door. By age 14, he owned a small international import business. He worked his way through college and graduate school as a retail salesperson, radio broadcaster, recreation manager, and a prison therapist. He earned his bachelor's degree from the University of Wisconsin in speech and political science, his master's degree from the University of Minnesota in communication and sociology, and his doctorate from the University of Minnesota in interpersonal communication and psychology, graduating with summa cum laude honors each time.

By age 21, he was teaching at the University of Minnesota, and during the next 15 years, he was selected as the "outstanding faculty member" by two different universities—Emporia State University and Minnesota State University-Mankato.

After 15 years of teaching, Dr. Zimmerman founded Zimmerman Communi-Care Network, Inc., a speaking, training, coaching, and consulting company, where he delivers more than 90 programs a year in the United States and internationally. As a prominent, sought-after speaker, Alan has delivered more than 3,000 keynotes and seminars for a variety of organizations and professional associations from Fortune 500 companies to small and medium-sized businesses, from state and federal government to education and health care groups.

As a prolific author, Dr. Zimmerman is the twenty-plus-year publisher of the *Tuesday Tip*, a weekly Internet newsletter that focuses on maximizing human performance, increasing leadership effectiveness, and developing communication competence. Some of his other books include *Pivot: How One Turn in Attitude Can Lead to Success*, and *Brave Questions: Building Stronger Relationships by Asking All the Right Questions*.

Dr. Zimmerman has received numerous awards and honors for his contributions in the fields of motivation, communication, and leadership. He has been twice selected as the most "distinguished faculty member" by the Institute for Management Studies. The National Speakers Association placed him in the Speaker Hall of Fame, awarding him its highest honor, the Council of Peers Award of Excellence (CPAE).

Among his avocations are biking, hiking, refinishing antique furniture, and participating in church activities. He and his wife Chris are world travelers, including tribal treks in Southeast Asia and visits to the Arctic, and split their time between their Florida and Colorado offices and homes. For additional information, visit www.DrZimmerman.com.

Index